CRYPTOGRAMS

PUZZLE BOOK FOR ADULTS

500 Large Print Cryptogram Puzzles To

Challenge Your Brain

Stephen J. Ellis

TABLE OF CONTENTS

HOW TO PLAY 1

TIPS 2

PUZZLES 5

HINTS 175

SOLUTIONS 185

HOW TO PLAY

A cryptogram is a popular puzzle game which is widely used for entertainment purposes. The puzzles are **short quotes and phrases** which are **encrypted** using a simple substitution code.

In this book, there are 500 cryptogram puzzles. Each puzzle is a quote made by a famous personality. <u>Each quote is encrypted in such a way that each letter of the alphabet is a substitute for another letter</u>.

For Example:

J NBVYHAE WE BLBWJBV PQBL J WTMB YQBW

WE GHJBLNV.

- TKHTQTW DJLFADL

The above is a cryptogram puzzle for the below quote…

I DESTROY MY ENEMIES WHEN I MAKE THEM

MY FRIENDS.

- ABRAHAM LINCOLN

In this example, the letter 'J' represents the letter 'I', 'N' represents 'D', 'B' represents 'E', and so on. Your **objective** is to figure out the code to solve each puzzle.

TIPS

So, you finally got hold of the new set of cryptogram puzzles that your peers were talking about. And you cannot wait to simply start to solve them!

But wait, all of these puzzles look a bit unnerving. How do you even start? Well, like any other kind of puzzle, there are some tactics.

Here are 8 tips for the beginner who is unsure of how to solve cryptogram puzzles.

1. One-Letter Words:

Always begin with the one-letter words in your cryptogram. After all, there are only a few letters that can be used as a word. The most common of these letters are **'a'** **and 'I'**. When you have these letters figured out, go on replacing the cipher (the substitute letter) throughout the cryptogram.

2. Most Commonly Used Letters:

In an English sentence, some letters repeat more frequently than others. So, to solve your cryptogram, look for the ciphers that occur at a higher frequency. More often than not, you should be able to decode these ciphers as one of the 6 letters, **E, T, A, O, I, and N**. And if you've already decoded 'I' and 'A' as in tip #1, this step moves forward quickly.

3. Double Letters:

Very few words have double letters in them, such as 'OO', or 'EE', or 'LL'. Examples include 'Door', 'Feel', 'Well', etc. So, look for the words that have double letters and try to decode the cipher. The easiest way to do this is to get your spelling brain activated and focusing on the letters that come before and after the double letters.

4. Contractions:

Contractions are a way to join two words with an apostrophe. They are used majorly in dialogues or extremely informal writing. Examples include **don't, won't, you're, she's, it's,** and so on . Spot these apostrophes and try to understand the letter appearing right next to each apostrophe. If you have possessive contractions, such as "man's", "cat's", or "tree's", it becomes easier to decipher the letter 's'.

5. Digraphs:

Some letters appear commonly in pairs. The best example is 'Th' in words such as 'Them', or 'They', or 'This'. The easiest would be to figure out a 'The' if you've already found out the cipher for the letter "e".

6. Two and Three-Letter Words:

These are the next words you should tackle in your cryptogram. Popular two-letter words include 'am', 'an', 'is', 'it', 'of', 'to', 'go', and so on. Three-letter words are a little tougher but if you can crack down common ones such as 'are', 'the', 'and', etc., solving the puzzle becomes a lot easier.

7. Unused Letters:

This trick comes in handy when you're almost done with the puzzle, yet cannot get the last bits straightened out. Take a good look at your semi-solved puzzle and think of the letters in the English alphabet that have not been used. Do any of them drill any sense into your unsolved sections? More often than not, they do!

8. Use a Pencil:

Guessing and making mistakes is a part of solving cryptograms. Use a pencil so you can correct your guesses if they're wrong.

Logic:

Lastly, you must apply your logic to solve the puzzle. And that's because, well, it's a puzzle and it's an exercise for your brain. You need to keep a cool head and apply pure logic to decode what's in front of you. And if you're playing at a contest and need to keep score, your cool head will matter much more than any of the above tricks.

So now, back to your puzzle and have a great time decoding the "secret message".

If Needed, Two HINTS For Each Puzzle Are Offered Starting On Page 175. If You Get Stuck On A Puzzle, The Complete SOLUTIONS For All Puzzles Start On Page 185.

PUZZLES

1.

SUFTGFTK FR IURH ABIT HZP OZT'G XTZA

BZA, NPG CIJH OFMMFVPDG ABIT HZP OZ.

- IOKUJ OIKUR

2.

PD MWGYPDJ, LDK XNAC FLLT ELW LW

ANASKZC CUGC CUKWK PA XLWK CUGD PA

ZGANGFFO AKKD.

- JKLWJK IWPMJXGD

3.

FLM NRJ'W NYKRW WYK DRHK. FLM NRJ'W

NYKRW WYK DBVJO. FLM DKW LMW TYRW

FLM CMW VJ RW WYK KJO LQ WYK ORF.

- ORGRGF

4.

TDXF PGJ'N GDKFNMPJL ADR CPJB. TDXF PG

GDKFNMPJL NMUN CPJBG ADR.

- TDOFNNU ADRJL

5.

H FIV VMRMP FDVXMVU UD KMHVB THFUIUMT

UD.

- EDAV UCNMP

6.

WC UYZ CBWPB BY RWKH YO BXS RWU, BXS

RWU WEESWPC.

- PZTV

7.

VCA BG RMKOBKO. LMJ KPIPC VCCBIP, TJA

LMJ FPPH OMBKO BK AZP ZMHP AZVA LMJ

YBRR.

- VKGPRX FBPQPC

8.

N RZLVMH LF FDXVDMV UGD QMDUF NWW

NKDEJ TDE NMH FJLWW WDCVF TDE.

- VWKVZJ GEKKNZH

9.

DJ JDY LJQWA IMJJCY B RNOYDAWYCC

YUOCSYDIY JD IJDAOSOJD JR MBZODK

BWW SMY JSMYN SMODKC OD SMY LJNWA.

– BNOCSJSWY

10.

YWV LFARCY AJ WLQQOCVZZ YWLY IAR

WLNV KVQVCKZ AC YWV LFARCY AJ

JHVVKAF IAR WLNV OC IARH WVLHY.

- YWOBW CWLY WLCW

11.

JNKDZ PG ZOB IUZOBX NI PSQBSZPNS.

- VUHPHBN VUHPHBP

12.

VZ VD'L F PWWO VOHF, PW FTHFO FAO OW

VD. VD'L HFLVHG DW FLQ ZWGPVBHAHLL

DTFA VD VL DW PHD IHGJVLLVWA.

- PGFUH TWIIHG

13.

NB IXZB JY LYCJOCSXMMD EB RSPGOCF YKK

LMOKKU XCT TBZBMYGOCF YSQ NOCFU YC

JIB NXD TYNC.

- VSQJ ZYCCBFSJ

14.

WCW FPIRKGV EGGQ AC EGGQ, JCRAP AC

JCRAP. LYA KNGIA JYVXF XV BXQG

BXAGNIAYNG.

- NIDX VPIRQIN

15.

OYMXSNMESX YA PIX PU MBX QPAM

YIMXSXAMYID NIWAYDIYUYLNIM

XVRSXAAYPIA PU BEQNIYMJ.

- R. M. FNSIEQ

16.

QJO BQIMVI QBQP AJWD OMV IWNZ OMV

RNIO WA VTVJPRQP ZSAV.

- CQYZW CSGQIIW

17.

VNZWAIRIFLZHR SPIFPNQQ WHQ DNPNRM

SPIULGNG KQ BLVW DIPN NTTLZLNAV

DNHAQ TIP FILAF YHZOBHPGQ.

- HRGIKQ WKERNM

18.

AVD WSVXYYDB VDDY FL WO WZAXBA

YXDB XO AVD VFCD AVWA VXB WZA XB

QFFR.

- HWCXY QTCAW

19.

LVYIFCNEYQ FIICN FH OHVCN. YX YN

NHKYXMCI CIKYSIVIC LVHZ XEI GFDMYNE HL

KHFIKYFINN.

- CGD EGZZGVNAWHKC

20.

VEF OFTKZSQ DI TNN QDDK ADDXG ZG

NZXF T MDSLFOGTVZDS BZVE VEF IZSFGV

CZSKG DI JTGV MFSVHOZFG.

- OFSF KFGMTOVFG

21.

KEPSFCEW VJTSF MPCEW AJT CL

UXTSKCEYP VJTSF YCOCEW AJT.

- BJLXQF FXYYXT

22.

MIBHB VHB UY HRWBJ GYH GHTBUZJITN.

TM ORJM QB WBGM MY TMJBWG. PB

SVUUYM GYHSB TM VULOYHB MIVU WYKB.

- PTWWTVO IVFWTMM

23.

IZCBQYIE KQFGNBP KIF TIRRCE ZNBC IEJ

ZNBC QEGN GKC KIEJF NT IYIJCZQYF.

- UNBC SQJIR

24.

TN AJ VJ OJNVUD, TN AJ VJ FHVNUYVBUN

HX ANXNUYF, VJ WN CJUTYUMNM THVQHX

JBUINFGNI.

- INYRBI QNYXND

25.

VFM SXVBCV BC DAV S LBGGMXMDV QBDL

AG YMXCAD, ZTV MHMXP YMXCAD BC S

LBGGMXMDV QBDL AG SXVBCV.

- MXBU KBOO

26.

WZ QTHB ELAWTYV WYVIWBC TANCBV AT

PBCEK KTBC, MCEBY KTBC, PT KTBC EYP

GCLTKC KTBC, QTH EBC E MCEPCB.

- RTNY EPEKV

27.

RUXHWUH XR OPH NDHFO FWOXGTOH OT

OPH JTXRTW TK HWOPZRXFRS FWG

RZJHDROXOXTW.

- FGFS RSXOP

28.

QU FMZ FQJQWR'P IQRMF NWO FMZ RDOP

NIZ EQFM KDX, PDJZFMQWR PBZGQNV

MNBBZWP.

- IQGL PBIQWRUQZVO

29.

 TUL IEH'C KMC ZLIG YUHM SH PSDM SD TUL UHPT

BUFW UH CGM YETA BGMH TUL DMMP

KUUY.

- VMFFT BMAC

30.

BC GPRUR'W M VAAT FAZ URMXXF IMSG GA

URMH, VZG BG PMWS'G VRRS IUBGGRS FRG,

GPRS FAZ KZWG IUBGR BG.

- GASB KAUUBWAS

31.

QWFHJ PORFU YFRFW QS SLJ. JDFX QS SY.

-TFYVHGOY DHWWOUSY

32.

OCSW DSQHX ICMWMLZSICR S XWZSPLH

TPGHPWTMP TXWCSW TWX IZTDSZR ZSO

DSWHZTSNX SZH NTLCW SPV WTDH.

- UMCP FHZLHZ

33.

MEZ'X WEF CZEG XIBAB QNZ'X ZE MBDNO,

NX'R PFRX LEM GIBZ IB'R MAFZC.

- XEV GQNXR

34.

NXMBJWR QJ WNB CQSJW HNOIWBS XC

WNB ZXXT LQJVXK.

- WNXKOJ UBCCBSJXM

35.

U IBAAIF KIUAAFMP CBII QYZZNMA U LUR

AJMNYXJ XMFUA KUABXYF.

- HULFQ LNRMNF

36.

ZN'R RB QZYO IYK EON RB NOSSZVAO NB

RNIYK ZY QSBYN BQ I VAIYF TIYLIR.

- CIXA TOHIYYO

37.

JUI VLKJ XK L KJIVVXWD KJQWI, WQJ L

OXRRKJQWI.

- EQZIEJ VRLWJ

38.

SYJEJ HC, BX VBZECJ, PB AFEUJE KFCC

YOCSJEHF HP FKJEHVFP YHCSBEO SYFP SYJ

JGHNJKHV BX EFVHCK.

- IJLHP OBZPU

39.

LHWFOPWMM NM F VGO GI MDFVV OENPLM

UGPW KWVV.

- HFB VWKNM

40.

VKLQIFLQV AKS GSI ZPEEV SG WKI IK

HQQG GQKGEQ KSI, MSI IK VQQ ZCK

YPDQV QWKSRC IK MDQPH ICQL NKZW.

- VKYDPIQV

41.

DXFGLAE OMFR MAR DXFGLAE NIMFH

NXISHLISN KMA US HDX RLCCSFSAH

HOLAEN.

- UTFXA RXFEMA

42.

IYB HIP WLOI XW'J ZYYP WY RHTJO XI YTM

RTMJTXW YA LHRRXIOJJ HIP NTJW GO

LHRRF.

-ZTXUUHTCO HRYUUXIHXMO

43.

K NGAB FH RA ZL ZOZFANJ KLYALFHJ PVAL K

PZG Z WKB. K'O ZDPZTG KLYALFKLE

GHOAFVKLE.

- ZDZL ZDBZ

44.

QX'C SGX BWQSAET XG DHTQKH QX. Q'L

OGLAGDXWUTH ZQXJ LI BGCQXQGS QS

WLHDQOWS JQCXGDI.

- DGPSHI YQSN

45.

LYT WSY BISVKEVEYA OBLIKOWSYOCEB EO GSI

RTKKTI KCSY 50 BITSVCEYA EK.

- FYMKT ILVFYT

46.

NPD VTN MJQOL NPD LOPB BJP NPDI IKTA

UIQKOYH TIK, SDM NPD BPO'M IKTAAN LOPB

DOMQA NPD JQM IPZL SPMMPV.

- DOLOPBO

47.

N KAZE WNHT IDZVUW YRGGD CNEY EYV

ZNIGUV EYNHJZ. RGGSVPNRENHJ EYV

XUVZZNHJZ JFT JROV IV.

- TIB

48.

ILYT QAO'DY DCRCTV, ATWQ KLY DNFY CT

ILCFL QAO'DY DCRCTV CG CJXADKNTK.

- PCWW GLAYJNMYD

49.

CBCOP OCHUYQQUHVC VGICQ NG NTC

XGOWE XYNT U VOP, NTC VOP GK NTC

TZIUH QAYOYN NG MC KOCC.

- UHHC QZWWYBUH

50.

WB KPC ZSWXG KPC SQUI WZ ZPCVS, JIQR

SWOZPJK YPPGO.

- YWEE NQSIJ

51.

M AWZL RTSL NT JLDMLZL NAWN RWQMXY

BTQ SUVLDBMV XTN VLDB-MXFODYLXN. MN

MV WX WRN TB VOQZMZWD.

- WOFQL DTQFL

52.

WVD SZPXY EFYW ID HZTHDKLDC SKWV

GKPD KT WVD YZFJ IFW DODHFWDC SKWV

HJKTKHQJ HZZJTDYY.

- BZQT EKPZ

53.

E AYN HIC YMSCD EM HIC KYVTDC YMX

PYVZCX LMHED E ACH IEK UVCC.

- KEPICDYMSCDF

54.

HPEPY JZKHO LR FWKH LY IWHAPY LY

PHPUKPC W ULUPHJ SLHAPY JZWH KC

HPBPCCWYQ JL RKAZJ JZPU.

- WQH YWHI

55.

EU'G RKGERY UD VD K HDO YEANU, UNKS

UD RBMCKES TNQ QDI VEVS'U.

- JKYUES XKS OIYRS

56.

DKOC ZCVO WKO BWVK ZP XBWOUFWIUO

VZGOH ZLOU F GFC, CZWKBCM VFC VIUO

BW EIW WKO HVUFWVKBCM ZP F YOC.

- HFGIOX XZLOU

57.

W'D HIZWEU HK OIWHR LKKMQ HYCH

HCQHR JWMR WXR XIRCD LGH YCBR HYR

EGHIWHWKE KS BRURHCLJRQ.

- ACE LIKOE

58.

SBR VWQ NM SBR FNWVT LACDRWIR CI

TNAH, OLSCS ORAUI SNYVWU GLISCQR.

– FVWSCA TLSBRW ZCAH, GW.

59.

CHF'B BAKFO MLHRB BAS YBMWB HV BAS

WMIS, BAKFO MLHRB BAS SFCKFJ.

- RYMKF LHPB

60.

OZMKM YA CD ZRJJYCMAA MQFMJO YC OZM

KMRGYBROYDC OZRO XM ZRTM

RFFDHJGYAZMV ADHMOZYCN.

- ZMCKU LDKV

61.

JBM FMPCGPAG FNJMO QA IJG QI IPTPM

UCNNQIF, VBG QI MQAQIF PTPMO GQWP LP

UCNN.

- EJIUBEQBA

62.

SYSBD PBURXU VRCX JRX NBFXJ RZ JRX

LMZ XLFE, PZV CPRZUX JRX LMZ ZPUFBS

RZUL JRX CRHUFBSX.

- JSZBD MPBV NSSHJSB

63.

D SJODJPJ IYKI K QGDJFIDQI OAAUDFV KI

FAFQGDJFIDHDG ELASOJRQ DQ CMQI KQ

XMRS KQ IYJ FJBI VMW.

- LDGYKLX E. HJWFRKF

64.

L NLZ ZLV ZAJDR'P KLRKJI AGP L QAAZ IXOJ.

UJJF QAXRQ.

- MXKCXJ RAMPAR

65.

ABBHJQU KCP RHSJKNA KJA CHQ ACHSNM

YLQMHSQ OSJOHUA KCP PLJARQLHC.

- VHMC B. XACCAPF

66.

RWGQCX QWG SEEAXJWQJSNOX IWNC JFG

LNNM UNAW XNAE SX TWSJSOP QLNAJ

UNA.

- CQWXFQ ONWCQO

67.

ZJCBC SYU Y ZOEC OT YECBOLYT JOUZIBF

SJCT YQEIUZ CMCBF SJOZC KCBUIT VTCS

SJI YBCZJY GBYTVQOT SYU.

- KCYDI DBFUIT

68.

G'KU CMP DCU TYJD YA PMN DCMD HYRZP

XMQU TD. AJMVOGT YA MTTGTG QGOQ

IMIGUT.

- PYREZMT MPMXT

69.

VSTLN KQ NJT VZKDN YC LO ZOOTITQQLSB

MLS.

-RYJO LALHQ

70.

HQARBXIR SIX IXSC, VKQRBR SIX IXSC,

BQQ. BKXE CTDX TARTYX JR, SAY

RQHXBTHXR BKXE ZTA.

- RBXLKXA PTAV

71.

Z DUCWY'X DUM U CWPT QJJM MUT. Z XDZYI Z

SZQDX AXZVV HW DGYQJCWP UYM WCWPTJYW'A

MWUM UYM ST PJJX HWWP'A QJYW.

- DJVVT H

72.

E RVSG EVRBIR BI OZR ZOG DXZ BI

BOIWBVGY, USR ZOG DXZ BOIWBVGI

ZRXGVI.

- IETJEYZV YETB

73.

QBUMWGUMQ GW'Q WRM PBLZJMT WRFW

WMFARMQ TBL F SBW FNBLW TBLZ

XMQWGJFWGBJ.

- XZFHM

74.

KBCCPXDVV ZDCDXZV RQJD QX GKD PXUBJZ

ZPVCQVPGPQX QS RPXZ GKBX QX QIGUBJZ

HPJHIRVGBXHDV.

- WDXNBRPX SJBXEYPX

75.

MRFN OCU LZPTU RFJRNU ICUEU OCUEU RJ

YWH PFNOCU YWH IRZZ SGEF WGO OCU

LPRF.

- YWJULC TPKLSUZZ

76.

BVST ZJZBKD ML V QHVSB WJI'CB KBCBY

FBBK.

-ZVYU LDYVKX

77.

EYK AROR QYOM BY QR C TVCERO. EYK

AROR HRCMB BY QR SROR. BSGJ HYHRMB

GJ EYKOJ.

- SROQ QOYYNJ

78.

CL NZTG BR YTGWTF NK XB AGJT DQ,

YGWT G VBBZ USTGJRGKX, GFZ KQTFZ XYT

STKX BR XYT ZGL ZSGANFV.

- QTXTS RGEJ

79.

DFQRJTQRD AFY VYDJ UHBR JF ZYJ FX ITZ

PIFDD HXM ZERJRXM JF KR ZDAOURM.

- QTXMA WHITXP

80.

YRZJ RT CY BFEHL FRDSEHP RH ZVLJY CY

YBORHP. GCB YRZJBEZJY EB EY DJBBEHP

PR.

- FJOZVH FJYYJ

81.

ZYTPDZ UO LAE LUWPD. NP VJGNTP. BYGP

UO GYD LUWPD. NP LFYZPBJT. SADSPUZ

UO OPTB LUWPD. NP SYFPBJT.

- QAVD KAAEPD

82.

EWTCATCZ GLKD CWAYLF TH CKA QKEPTCZ

AUF KOXFQA, TA'H LFWVTHTCZ KCF'H

HFCHWATKCH.

-EWYV QFNWCCF

83.

EJH FUCREHM JUK EJH SRCYHMKH CR JCK

PCRZ URZ JURZK.

- VHLRUMZL ZU YCRAC

84.

WFTNT BH RY HVZHWBWVWT EYN ZYYUH

BR WFT SBET YE Q MFBSX.

- AQNG TSSTR MFQHT

85.

FCA'SO IOBOS N TCXOS AIUQT FCA EAQU

USFQIW.

- KQGO PQUGN

86.

JFX BXPE ADDGJ PJ DHX RDCWE ABXPLFX

PUB, LD QUWW CI PHE WUNX.

- PHHUX EUWWPBE

87.

RXD UHXQ, BXMMNK, KXGN STRK NPNH GR

JDIUR FXIUNZKBAE DHSNFETHZK SXH'Z

BNJE.

- MAJJ QTZZNFKXH

88.

SZI TOPTCKIRICS TCO OFJJWYFUC UJ

QCUMXIONI FY SZI UCXE NWTDOFTC UJ

SDWI XFVIDSE.

- LTRIY RTOFYUC

89.

N DH D KSBF FDSOLZ, EPC N XLYLZ FDSO

EDUOFDZRK.

- DEZDJDH SNXUBSX

90.

GE QLI RLQCOJ LAUB'O GE OCONU. GE

JOAUBYORJ LBI GE OLNUBO LAU GE OCONU.

- NLEBU JOLNUE

91.

QNR KRYJRQ TX NMIIBWRKK BK QT YTSWQ

ETSJ GURKKBWFK VNBUR TQNRJK MJR

MCCBWF SI QNRBJ QJTSGURK.

- VBUUBMZ IRWW

92.

UZ UD HWZ ZLB DUSB WA G FGH YNZ ZLB

DUSB WA LUD LBGCZ ZLGZ FGZZBCD.

- BMGHPBC LWRKAUBRP

93.

QCAXFGAXQ, BITF KCP'HX NCCEGYZ LCH GQ

TNHXTUK FIXHX.

- THXFIT LHTYENGY

94.

EIF RAKFDE RW NRZF TB ER BFXZF, VRE ER

GTV.

-GRRPXRG GTNBRV

95.

WM'E IKM MGP JPEMWITMWKI MGTM

OTMMPYE. WM'E MGP ZGTISP KU EZPIP.

- AYWTI PIK

96.

PFYFYIFP SRLS RLJJTDFBB TB L GLQ EX

SPLCFM,DES L AFBSTDLSTED.

- PEQ VEEAYLD

97.

MQY TSM NQTFFYIPYL MQY MYNQIAFAPH,

TIX MQY MYNQIAFAPH GILUGSYL MQY TSM.

- KAQI FTLLYMYS

98.

N OXPOJX ZUQGPRQ QGX TMPZJXKSX PE

QGXUW ONVQ GUVQPWF, PWUSUM NMK

ARJQRWX UV JUTX N QWXX ZUQGPRQ

WPPQV.

- YNWARV SNWDXF

99.

DEFJ PWWG ZLOSZ. WKWNVULIV ZWJF

UWJJWN OX JRWV PWWG MJ OJ.

- JWI HOQQOMBF

100.

HUHMZNPH ODJTHT JXBHM DJFFSPHTT, PNB

PNBSOSPL BDJB DJFFSPHTT ST MSLDB JB

BDHSM DHHGT.

- QHMBNGB QMHODB

101.

EJ ZAAWFLI FLNA XAKG MGNRFZY AT

RXGKFDRL OFYNAKJ, BG DRL XRWG XAKG

YGLYG AT BORN'Y ORQQGLFLI NAMRJ.

- DOKFYNAQO BRZNH

102.

J BOJQOHUYGX GU UEAOEZO IYE NHGZKU

XOEXBO WEKOWYOH.

- KOEHKO I. NDUY

103.

DQTKUAQPA DI E TAUDYWOGFU ZFO

TDIOSAIIDQY IOEOA, NA LFIO ZA TKDQY

IKLAOWDQY OK ZA WECCH.

- LEWEOLE YEQTWD

104.

MWF IOXVK BWK DT SDQT KW WFKKVOBG,

WFK ISHGTK WH WFKRLTBJ MWFH

YWILTKOKOWB, DFK MWF YSB WFKPWHG

KVTI.

- QWF VWQKA

105.

UK RUM PMRP ZMTJIKPG, JKFNP

AJVKQWPUVN. UK RUM NHFQIP SVQWQKPP,

LFIUKJP HMBK.- PFVQI DFPVH

106.

YSSXL UJF ZPF YQFLLFC OPQSJSISJW SI

ZPF WMKC.

- SLGUQC OPUWYFJL

107.

ESP ISFGP IPXEICMK PVNCDXRFD QUES RX

XPPD CX MFQCDERH. JLE RE'X C YFBP, C

JGFE FD CQPMRHCD SRXEFMU.

- AMCDB ICEPMX

108.

WYU KHTW YIKMZ WYJZP MCHIW IT JT HIS

WUBYZHEHPF.

- KMSTYMEE KBEIYMZ

109.

W NYZXI DYXGIWIZ OSXO OSELY KSE XGY

SXJJWYLO XGY OSELY KSE ME OSY RELO

CEG EOSYGL.

- NEEPYG O. KXLSWIZOEI

110.

YTXD ADRBM CZEG RGC QJIMODM BOD MZIY

RGC RJB JDNTGCM VZI BORB VZI ORLD ZGD.

- MBDYYR RCYDJ

111.

KSZANEL SZ X WXBF NP CSUZ TU WCXL ND

AKU VUXV.

- YNCAXSEU

112.

FRDFTR MPR APMFFRW EC SEHADPL MCW

SEHADPL EH APMFFRW EC ASRO.

- GMORH KMTWVEC

113.

HUZ BZSE JBFIEZW KM PFH CUZHUZB

WSQUKPZM HUKPR IYH CUZHUZB WZP XF.

- I. T. MRKPPZB

114.

U HCG SUB NOB UNDOBP MTG EDNHP

FGJDNG MTG MNOMT SUB LGM CMK FDDMK

DB.

- XUVGK EUMM

115.

UQMFXUO DCU YXP MFJ KXOFM MFCM

AFXUJA NWQPVXMFXU.

- PCIC CUOJKQG

116.

EOONKGCENO EU CAS NRCQNXS NM G

AGJEC,ONC G WGOLNX GQC.

- URFGOC WGCOGFGW

117.

D CUJH VLY QUDMHZ. D CUJH TSXY QLSVZ

10,000 KUPX YCUY KLV'Y KLNG.

- YCLWUX HZDXLV

118.

KGN IEEFVHR JEN ZKG HWKUS EG K

JXXWFX, JMW KFF WRX SPEIXHHEPH VG

WRX TEPFL ZKGGEW UKCX K JXXWFX.

- KPWRMP HZRESXGRKMXP

119.

BKWF JHY'PW GWWF IWJHFO JHYXGWMA,

SKWF JHY VCJ ALFO, DWCTW HA VLFO LG

BCLSLFQ SKWXW.

– QWHXQW KCXXLGHF

120.

VZ QCSLRRC LRG DKKSIAAVDR FDTI QD

QPVA XLRG VQ JVXX EI VR QPI MYVAI DZ

ZVMPQVRM L ZDSIVMR IRITC.

- HLTIA TLGVADR

121.

VQZSOJVU FJUB UBY GZJUYM PUIUYP JP

QZY QS UBYQDYHFBYOAJZW SIVUP QS

OIUJZ IAYHJVIZ BJPUQHK.

- PUYXBYZ TJZNYH

122.

DOBEVPOC EVDE LXO'E HFQQ, P IXO'E LDOE

EX POZFOE. PEH HDQF PH NYXXG XG

SEPQPEB, DOI SEPQPEB PH HSKKFHH.

- EVXADH FIPHXO

123.

SZFFTJXOO TO JMV OMIXVSTJA KMB

FMOVFMJX DME VSX DBVBEX. TV TO

OMIXVSTJA KMB PXOTAJ DME VSX FEXOXJV.

- CTI EMSJ

124.

WM UNP FWMG JK PZPQB YQUWCU UNPQP

WC Y FYCUPQEWPTP.

- DYW AQPPMP

125.

VB AMAJWEPVIT VD TGX'D ZVFF, EPAI DG VD

EPA VIMAIEVGI GB EPA MKUUVIA, NHDE

FVRA EPA DAKEQAFE.

- AFD QGJDE

126.

DFGBSLTLKP RN XSPDBRSK DBXD MXNS'D

XELWSZ MBFS PLW MFEF HLES.

- XTXS YXP

127.

BECDVED CB XJOCE MUJM HZFIB.

- IKFM RZVVDOKM

128.

EF FZAHG Z WPHZF CHZD TM BEGFTPQ FT

VPTCNYH Z DEFFDH DEFHPZFNPH.

- BHSPQ LZOHG

129.

UZ RHI NH LAQ PHJC RHI YQL JQPWJNQN.

LAQJQ WJQ OH TAHJLKILT UO MUZQ.

- BUKAWQM XHJNWO

130.

OUP EHMLQGOSHL HE GXX OPTULHXHRW SV

ESIP.

-SVGGT GVSKHF

131.

IMZOZ C DZI KDEZDGKAD XOANKHZH GA JZ

QHZPQV, KG AQFMG GA JZ GOKZW.

- GMANCH SZPPZOHAD

132.

GUJ'C OSICB VUPA CYHB UJ EBSZUPIV,

IUHBCYHBI VUP'AB SMBSG, IUHBCYHBI

VUP'AB QBMYJG.

– HSAV IWMHYWM

133.

CXPA VWBA OT VOEA RYWTCT, FYOMY

ABAXNWZA CIVET ISWPC IZQ DAF YIBA

TAAZ.

- DXIZMWOT QA VI XWMYADWPMIPVQ

134.

OTZJZ'K KM WNBT RS FWZJRBFS TRKOMJD

OTFO TFK XZZS TRCCZS FSC KTNSSZC.

- FKTOMS KFSCZJK

135.

G AGWIH AKSHON GON G ILGNPR GDDHON

POWF RLSWH DLH IBO ILSOHI.

- XHOMGUSO AKGOYWSO

136.

PHHTYC HC DMKYC YQYT KGY SMPKYPK

CLTTYCP GMQY KH PKMTF MTF SEWGK.

- PKYXGYT VETW

137.

OXQJTBIBMG RE OJX PTZQP BU EB

ZDDZTMRTM OJX CBDIK OJZO CX KBT'O JZFX

OB XLVXDRXTQX RO.

- SZL UDREQJ

138.

ZVDXD'L INNT CM DPDXAYNTA. YNNLZ.TNM'Z

FMNHF.

- UGXXDM I. VGXTCMI

139.

AV EUVZ VKMQWSMV MVFNIEPECO QI MNV

KNEZM MVZW SIH TIHVZ VKMQWSMV

MVFNIEPECO QI MNV PEIC MVZW.

- SZMNTZ FPSZDV

140.

PCSGD RAC GIPCO PJBC S TGX, OX NXI QSD

YGCSB RACH PJBC SD SGRJOR.

- TSYPX TJQSOOX

141.

RU FAH UKKJ XAAO BCAHP EQA FAH BLK

RWTROK, RP ERJJ LBORBPK.

- ZBPPR TGRPQ

142.

GZLFZU WEC HFY VZ VLEPZL YGEH EHCFHZ

ZJUZ. YGZC'LZ ISUY VLEPZL QTPZ WTHSYZU

JFHMZL.

- LFHEJA LZEMEH

143.

MF TDF QUIZN MSUL UFZLGCOCYB MLFG
MLTU MF DFTOOB MTGU SQ RIQU QUIEE
ULTU MCDNQ.

-PCIYOTQ TPTKQ

144.

V KWD'L PBDL LW DBIX IR ABDKWI, V PBDL
LZXI LW DBIX LZXITXMYXT. VA V'I QWWM
PVLZ VL, V'I QWWM PVLZ VL.

- KWSB QBL

145.

CWX MYCEIC IXXI BWMC UCWXYI URSA
NMCNW MTSEJGIX UH.

- SXURMYQU QM KERNE

146.

OJ BHZGJMZ HMQ VHDN. MS SMJ VHM VHZVX

H RGAX PGZX HMLJE.

- XJEOJEZ XSSYJE

147.

L QBTZ WBJZXY JN IXZ OKI OLVAN IX L

YJWWZBZXQ ELQK, UTQ VJHKQN QKZ OLM

OKZX YLBAXZNN PIXPZLVN MITB YLM.

- YIYJXNAM

148.

ZKMGEKG LERTZ ER KRSEIWP, NGKCSZG

LERTUGJAG NGUREAZ IR OSQCEMIP, CEJ

MZ IOG IRWKO TOMKO MUUSQMECIGZ IOG

TRWUJ.

- URSMZ Y

149.

FWKPOBPS UTKO VQR CMQU KMZ BO UBYY

TSYF VQR OQ JKCS PYSKW UTKO VQR ZQ

MQO CMQU.

- WSJNWKMZO

150.

D KHSDP DKS XV MEPSHDPNHS EY

QSHWDQY DMFDUY D KHSDP DKS XV

PHDIYMDPEXIY.

- SLHD QXNIA

151.

PMU BCDVAMU DCM KP IVU ZPLY PN NANIX

PLKAMCLX BUM. MP BCDVAMU DCM KP IVU

ZPLY PN PMU URILCPLKAMCLX BCM.

- UQFULI VJFFCLK

152.

XCQ CWVCQJX KHORYWOQZX XCGX BHN

KGZ RGB OQ WJ XH JGB XCGX W DHUP CGUI

QMQUB IGB, XCGX W ZQMQU IHV WX.

- DGBZQ VUQXFPB

153.

CEUMEHCBE FTMRJFFBRMR CLDICEDHCBE

NJH RVBJAZ EBH NM OBEGJRMZ SCHV CH.

- CIBT RHTDUCERYP

154.

O MCFOCUC OG ESC RCUOF. O MCFOCUC

ESCQC'V L DAR, EAA. O JCE DAR LE ZSTQZS

- ESC ZLESAFOZ ZSTQZS.

- EQOYYOC QCRR

155.

XUB NQL INDDJLYC MIJKL XUB NQL TNSJPZ

CIL ZQLNCLYC AUPCQJFBCJUP.

- QUFLQC G. SLPPLRX

156.

FQR PSBR OSL FM HMNUTR LMND JMYRL ZP

FM BMTH ZF MGRD MYAR SYH WNF ZF ZY

LMND WMACRF.

- CZYQNUUSDH

157.

S CZZR EWKJZHK YZZTN WN BWTA S YZPU

EWKJZHK S NZHB.

- RSCLHN KHBBWHN LWLACZ

158.

ECORE WOC ISPCE BZ EIS RSPR UPEUI

ZBCS, FBHS NJ FWHS EIWOKI EIS REPCR

APFM NPUMAPCYR.

- S.S. UOXXBQKR

159.

S RKP'A ADSPT ZEKYA ASLO. MKY'XO DOXO

IDOP MKY'XO DOXO. S ADSPT ZEKYA AKRZM,

FAZMSPC SP AYPO.

- GKDP JOO DKKTOX

160.

XDCTG XFKPDIK WNKFDLG WCB KPB

WGGWGGFLG DYFTBWSFGE.

- PBCJBCK PDDABC

161.

QCDTHVAIDY DA U RPCV, XIT ETCM ADLIX PQ

RIDSI DH YCDHX FUWTA XIT ITUCX RUCF.

- UOLOAXDHT GDCCTKK

162.

FQ FC KDJDX'C QBJ WAFYB C. QOJXVKBJCA,

FXPDXCBJ BQ CP, KD'G VCFYY ID DOCFXU

QJBHDX JOGFB GFXXDJV.

- SBAXXM ZOJVBX

163.

YDMVQ RDFJY HDAFIXO JDF WJDX YP

HAIX, XAHHASMVY YP VFJGF, JIX

ALBPOOAZVF YP HPDRFY.

- R. DJIXPVH

164.

ON WQO GINCZA PGEQBP NCK

COLTPKGLSLPG JLSINCS HONJLOV INJ

ZLSSZP IP HONJG.

- X. KNRPKS NBBPOIPLWPK

165.

ZHIHA RDYVH D BQZPVH VMQZGQZO DTEPV

KHEKSH UEP LEZ'V SQGH.

- LRQOMV L. HQYHZMERHA

166.

EO HSO HTT DI CJO ZQCCOS, UQC NGFO GV

QN HSO TGGRDIZ HC CJO NCHSN.

- GNWHS EDTLO

167.

YREHHBY IHA'P PCQRE QLCUNRQA ENYPHUZ PEQP OCBB, CYDCRNQBBZ Q BHP HM XBQRG QLCUNRQA ENYPHUZ.

- RHBYHA OENPCECQI

168.

ZCI YG XIHEOMJ OP HM HLLGYFL LC SMXGIPLHMX EKHL O ZGGU HDCSL LKG ECIUX O UOBG OM.

- DIOHM ZICSX

169.

PZA LJYXK FXLFWQ QAAVQ HYROZPAY LZAB WJT'DA MTQP VFKA QJVAPZRBO PZFP LFQB'P PZAYA HAUJYA.

- BARX OFRVFB

170.

M KHXHE QMFS CQ TK MLHI BMLNRCL

LNMKSMKV RG NRB M IMVNL MIQERXH ML.

- LNRITW T. HJMWRK

171.

UIUZJ HYYGPLDOMQPUAR MRHZRM KORQ

RQU WUYOMOGA RG RZJ.

- SGQA B. FUAAUWJ

172.

HJ SQR NVCQS DFN JYGAYGVBN QJ G

YQIN, SQR WRID GBBNLD DFN DFQYVI

OFHBF HD TNGYI.

- HIGGB FGSNI

173.

VFSSZHJCC ZC HTN F LFNNJD TR JYJHNC, ZN

IJSJHIC ESTH NVJ NZIJC TR NVJ LZHI.

- FMZQJ LJBHJMM

174.

XIK GUOKWXOGX OG WVX M QKDGVW NIV

COPKG XIK DOCIX MWGNKDG, IK OG VWK NIV

MGLG XIK DOCIX YBKGXOVWG.

- UTMBSK TKPO-GXDMBGG

175.

JXYXT HVXCNOAJ MJANBXT WMJ'C WANOYX.

BOC ROCQAW, GXC, KVN JAN BOC

WANOYXC.

- QROIBN Q. XOCXJBARXT

176.

MGPALBE ZPNVI OST IVV RFLBEI JHVPGVG,

PBM JHVPGVG PBM JHVPGVG IRLHH, TBRLH

OSTG VOVI PJFV.

- MPYLM FSJNBVO

177.

ERNTN DG AVERDAH VA ERDG NYTER QVTN

EV FN STDKNJ ERYA ETPN XTDNAJGRDS.

- ERVQYG YIPDAYG

178.

NB'Q NF XNBLJVBTJL BWVB BJTL XNML UVF

SL MDTFE. NB'Q TFELJ BWL YVQG DM

MNUBNDF BWVB HDT UVF BLXX BWL BJTBW.

- AVD C

179.

OIWREOL JFI ZBZ FJY AEFY YJ XI DJMIZ LJ

UCPR EL YJ XI CFZIWLYJJZ.

- QIJWQI JWAIDD

180.

DWN JKOQNGO XZP MND TGZH YBDNGJDPGN

FNINKF ZK DWN RPNODBZKO XZP IZON.

- HJGMJGND JDQZZF

181.

MFER ZQQBI KS FQEAR EMEZQ VI

PWCWJAYJC IVCQTPQ.

- PCEJNQ KWTQR

182.

G'T LFS X EXL FE OKCIGB UBYFFI XS XII. G

SYGLH GS'U FLR FE SYR WMRXSRUS

BXSXUSMFOYRU FE XTRMGBXL YGUSFMQ.

- HMU FLR

183.

OHS YCB'P WBHYW HB HTTHKPSBDPO'V

AHHK CBA BHP NI KICAO.

- NKSBH GCKV

184.

DRR LOFDXEPF HFNHRF JDVX XN ZN XTF

IVFKHFLXFZ.

- TFZQ RDCDOO

185.

EV EU APOI ZSTP ZT XFT PA OAPYTF

DTXFDWO VSXV ZT QTYEP VA MFTXVT.

- C. J. Z. VWFPTF

186.

NQVWKQW QBK KWOWU NYSOW YKW

DUYLSWZ TVAPYRA UBVNVKI AWK ZYUW

DUYLSWZN.

– IWYUIW LWUKBUJ NPBT

187.

ECUA KU NHCUYU KTY FKWY HO UAHGYU, UH

JU ULJYGLY FKWY HO OKLAU.

- NYGTJ RHJGLKTY

188.

KOS GSIK JUWSUKJVUI CBS NINCEEH YCXS

GH VNKIJXSBI NUCTCBS VR TOCK "ACU'K GS

XVUS".

-YCBKJU YCUU

189.

NDBGMVW MF B SIVCDNFBZMIV. BEE PIIHF

ZBEH. PQZ B WIIG PIIH EMFZDVF BF RDEE.

-UBNH YBGGIV

190.

ZOKKW BOKEF LKCFU HXF JXFFOU KR

XDUHKIM.

-LBIHDE OYHXFI

191.

YMYCL IZPUGCY OQNFO E OINU FZUQ FQZPQ UQY ECUZOU QEO REHHYX ZX HNMY.

- EHRCYJ OZOHYL

192.

ZDE'N WF PKODKE EFXFGGFS PKNEDBY FV SFGGJPKW BRFCE SABE ABHHDKDY JDNEDGYBJ.

- NEDOD QFRN

193.

DL'P EGEVDQC YWEL MIS AEQ EAAIGOUDPW DB MIS NI QIL AEXJ YWI CJLP LWJ AXJNDL.

- WEXXM P. LXSGEQ

194.

QYEJPWU YE VCWCGU O GYEJ PS

EIWLWYECE. YJ BOM PMGU LWCLOWC IE JP

KC EIWLWYECZ UCJ ODOYM.

- XIWJ FPMMCDIJ

195.

EUI ZCBBIKIGMIR JIEXIIG BKCIGZR MDGGTE

JOE KICGBTKMI EUICK BKCIGZRUCH.

– VDT ERI-EOGA

196.

HNGQABLOM ECCA ADGUBOV ZOFBD FNCU

VCF BF WBVNF.

- PBDDBC ICGO EBOV

197.

QHGSRNA HW HB PUQHBL XRBO ARCN

YOWS. HV ARC'QO XRBO ARCN YOWS,

ARC'QO JRB.

- YHFFA YRJONIUB

198.

KH HCJLX C UOLCH FLCV PA GPDOCUL HP

XLL HML QPOVF KT CVV KHX HCKTHLF

UVPOZ, CTF XHKVV VPBL KH.

- PXGCO QKVFL

199.

AL AFII MNDL N RZRNI HMNZU AFRMZOR

VZZSU, IFRLPNROPL, NYC IFVPNPW.

- NYYL ANICJNY

200.

CIS MGPU DBU GMC CM CILGA BHMFC

OMGSU LE CM IBKS B YQSBC NSBP MW LC.

- SNLCI DIBQCMG

201.

G MBQ VI MABQDIS VW CABF ABKKIQU FY XI.

VNF G JIPNUI FY VI JISNMIS VW GF.

- XBWB BQDIHYN

202.

JRD IMFXIU EZM TD JRD KAHQDUJ GAXIDU

THJ X LYAEXUD MAH JRDM PXKK ZIIAELKXUR

JRD KDZUJ.

-TZYZIS ATZEZ

203.

G WHR'Z ISNR HR UOGRK WGFNIIHGRZOW.

EO ISNR HR UOGRK QONSSP KHHW, NRW

HUTGHCFSP, EO ISNR HR EGRRGRK.

- KQOKK ZQHP

204.

DTOWHOWL OY XIYH TWNHERZ FTM NC

VRRDOWL T SOTZM.

- DTQGN DOJTYYN

205.

XLTJL KIYGRKF VIB YISIBBIE EGRNG NTK AL

MIKL YIMTP.

- TABTGTS XRKNIXK

206.

HKQWS VPQDYQ PVPO GIRH LDY QRKT LDY

XKQL RG YEYIOXPO TWGY.

- NYILDRTX PKYINPSD

207.

HENFN TQ KM 20 VNRF GNFTMI TK

RWNFTSRK ETQHMFV UENK QHMSBQ YMQH

WMKNV.

- G. D. M'FMPFBN

208.

ZI QSO NBVHUB SMMSYYZEWYA HNRZHLO

IQSI HLP IBVQEHYHWA QSO BGVBBFBF HLP

QLUSEZIA.

- SYNBPI BZEOIBZE

209.

HRM TMA HZ KDXXMKK CZY MOMYAHRNUF

NU WDKNUMKK, KXNMUXM QUG

HMXRUZPZFA NK UMOMY HZ CZPPZJ HRM

ZHRMYK.

- SQKQYD NWDTQ

210.

DYBFPTDJ RPNBFDNWFB QDK DRMDGK

CBBJ PYYPOFDJN.

- KDRYDJ FWKQUPB

211.

MFKHEAEJFZP WV UAD JUOUABU WU

HKFZWYHU CWVDAZP.

- KWYCHFX GFUUFD

212.

HLSMCFV VXBA UXMSL KBGM SC USRMV BH

ULBJEKM, CBU SC XZNNSCMVV.

- MJLSNSFMV

213.

XVND LIK PI IKF, PI IKF XOFV Y AYDP,

YDLFVODP LIK TI.

- SZYLAIO GYQFO

214.

SWDPWCSWZ SH M ENUGSWMCSNW NO

GBMSWH MWT UMCPBSMVH. CAP UNBP

GBMSWH INK KHP, CAP VPHH UMCPBSMV

INK WPPT.

- EAMBVPH O.

215.

HZSZI VQIIL NOQXU OZEHM QORZRRESZ. E
JEGZ QORZRRESZ CZQCJZ. QORZRRESZ
CZQCJZ FNGZ MIZNU NIU.

- RXRNH RQHUNM

216.

LTQESERTYKT KXY KAXYVT GXSJWQT
SYRD TIRQXDQBSYXQN XKASTHTPTYR.

- PXRR OSDYBS

217.

XQR YNL FS YDX NI XF DRHDRIRTX TFX XQR
FVXEYDB YHHRYDYTAR FS XQNTZI, WVX
XQRND NTEYDB INZTNSNAYTAR.

- YDNIXFXGR

218.

QEBRDER BQ N EUHHREYBUD UO

QSEERQQOSH PREBXRQ.

- XNSH ZNHRPG

219.

K'N ZYXHOKDV UFH BYOAU TOHAKIHDU KD

QNHOKZQD FKAUYOE.

- FHSHD UFYNQA

220.

RQI AZWW UVOVJ RZOV DQG SUDBXZUR DQG

FSU'BXSUIWV, EQ IQU'B EBJVEE.

— CVWWD FWSJCEQU

221.

K VBF'S TALV PBBYE PZ WABWOA DGB

GLHA PASTLZAV SGA XBSGATOLFV.

- HOLVKXKT WJSKF

222.

TLYMS FKLVD MLY RYLJKLAYZ GKS WN

DSLYGTSE WXS WN RYLDYQYLMGOY.

- DMAXYP UKEGDKG

223.

Z GSZR IGCSMU CE KMS HNK HZRYE CM

HNSM BNS GSEB KI BNS HKGRU HZRYE KAB.

- HZRBSG HCMDNSRR

224.

NJJ IU ZQXRSQR XZ SILTXSA KIVR LTNS

LTR VRUXSRKRSL IU RORVDCND

LTXSYXSA.

- NJFRVL RXSZLRXS

225.

BH EYFP AHK EFLP PH POA BHRLX. PFQM

EYFPMUMO AHK XMP HKP HI RP FLB YFUM

IKL.

- V YHGM

226.

UNV WKC XND FA AXFWWFCZ KZKFCAU

UNV AUQVKW ICDXA UNV AUQVCZUN DL

FU.

- XDDGQDX XFMADC

227.

LSKQAYOYWU OGFS PCL GJ P JYPCGAW

SVSCKGJS YB LQS QMZPA GZPWGAPLGYA.

- EPAGSO TSOO

228.

CE GUFB NEQ WFD, GABU GUFB NEQ UFLR,

GURIR NEQ FIR.

- BURECEIR IEEHRLRJB

229.

WFTD ZDMVWP RK QSW SY WPD OSHXDW,

CTW SY WPD PDMFW MQA SY WPD BRQA.

- XDIRQ NMWDK

CRYPTOGRAMS

230.

UXWIUP YPXWU JAKUWIXFS YAPWI

PUMLXFS AP LA JAKUWIXFS YAPWI

YPXWXFS.

- CUFZMKXF NPMFHGXF

231.

REKQPEQ KR J FDPGQSXIM HNKPL KX DPQ

GDQR PDH NJYQ HD QJSP DPQ'R MKYKPL

JH KH.

- JMVQSH QKPRHQKP

232.

NV KVD URS R FRS SRK. IAGI AL RNASM

ROS FM YTRLMHDB HVT VOM BMNN FRS

SRK LV JRNN LUTVDYU.

- TAGUMBBM M. YVVSTAGU

233.

KUM LZMIWMDK RIA HVKC KUM SVHEMWDM

HD KUWCSJU I XCWMDK RHZQMWVMDD.

- PCUV GSHW

234.

VZC ZNI EKVE SNF CNZ'E KVGH EN UH

THQJHYE, SNF YVZ UH ONNC.

- DNKZ LEHAZUHYP

235.

MNLA UCEBKA CO AWTE ILNX LOZ ZLEP. RP

GCKZ NGW XWTEM L ZLA.

- ILTK DLTDTCO

236.

PRORNW GPRAR ML ZBH AGLZ

RFZMPXLMFHLL TOHLMYHFZ MF R

QHFHORZMGF, THOBRTL MF RAHOMNRF

BMLZGOI.

- YMFHLB Y'LGXER

237.

OMYV DZIDXZ CRZ MF 25 MYC MKZY'F

UEKRZC EYFRX FSZV MKZ 75.

- UZYHMORY BKMYWXRY

238.

ZU'K AIMC HN NIZUD UDIU WICBK RBHRAB

INOIZQ HN WBBUZGL MDIAABGLBK, IGQ Z

VBAZBSBQ ZG WPKBAN.

- WFDIWWIQ IAZ

239.

RZUFV IKERUSY U IUDXTNVK RZEG U KVEFFJ

RESG GT DEJ.

- IEKUT HT

240.

JB'I LYB EKXB VYW ZYYF XB BKXB SXBBOTI,

JB'I EKXB VYW IOO.

- KOLTV CXUJC BKYTOXW

241.

ABC IQCCMYU IHXL JP X RYNCQIWH,

RBOPJGXH QCUJDMCQ YI YDC YI ABC

MXQZCPA MXOP JD XUCQJGXD BJPAYQO.

- XKJLXJH PRXDKCQLCQ

242.

QDGLV KXOMSCJ XO GBICXLGZ KXOMSCJ.

JSR LGZZSM MIDD SZI OMSCJ PXMKSRM

MIDDXZY MKI SMKIC.

- PXDDXGB QGCC

243.

XVDR SZJSPZ LGPP LVPQ GD VDE JWU JK

RJWY PGKZ,AWU JDPR UYWZ KYGZDEO

LGPP PZVNZ KJJUSYGDUO GD RJWY IZVYU.

- ZPZVDJY Y

244.

NEXP G NDI UAWPJXF, G NDI DYNDUI

MDWJEM PAM MA ZDTX XLOWIXI.

- CXFXT BXMXF

245.

ENJPJUJP VNJI MCPD MAAHB VNJI EQSS

YSBA, QD VNJ JDT, MCPD NCWYD MJQDRB.

- NJQDPQXN NJQDJ

246.

EF PWIIDO IQD NTONXPLIWENDL IQWI AFX

PWA GD ZFTEZ IQOFXZQ, SXLI HXLQ

IQOFXZQ TI.

- OWA CDKTL

247.

OIQ LGMQZGQ JD OJSWP ML OIQ

OQGIZJKJYP JD OJFJUUJH.

- QSHWUS OQKKQU

248.

HT CTWX, HT NMZXHGDOZF EBH EMTDD SOX

FBSO TNTVM GXDSZHA KZSOTVS CXBWZHI

DTJX JBMU TH ZS NTMXWXM.

- NMBHETZD JBVMZBE

249.

EQZT DWBZUQOTI OD OBRWAUVTU ZTWMIQ, LWM

YW OU ZKZT ON UQZ WYYD VAZ TWU OT

LWMA NVKWA.

- ZPWT BMDF

250.

XTOAO ZG CJDCFG GPBOXTZSM JOLX XP

JPHO.

- MCQAZOJ MCAVC BAUWOI

251.

VS'J LHSSHQ SU PDVW DVIVTE KVEK SKDT

SU JBYYHHX DVIVTE WUN.

- LVWW TVYKUWJUT

252.

QC QY QL AQCNGMCXGN CIMC CIN

BRLBGNCN RXCARRO RT IXKMLQCZ

GNBNQPNY QCY NHVGNYYQRL.

- MATGNJ LRGCI SIQCNINMJ

253.

Y EX E STQBGEKYSBTGR XVWW ONB Y WVV

YB EW XR JGVGTDEBYHV BT SFEQDV XR

XTTK AYUV BFV PVEBFVG.

- WFYGAVR XEQWTQ

254.

FRJ OGW QRM RGT WM TJWTJ MK RETFMCV,

ET ZEXJ G OGW QRM RGT WM JGCT MC

JVJT.

- GHMZK REFZJC

255.

HLU EOR CEWG, XFH RPO'H CEWG HP HLU.

- BPAO NFWOYU ERESZ

256.

LMT GKUY NM YBCYIN NGDFPX MW

LMTVXYJW QYWMVY LMT IKF RM NGYZ.

- ZDIGKYJ OMVRKF

257.

UAEBVMIGRUF HUVB GLIF AUUQE IFT
BKWBVRBFXB HUVB GLIF WBVEUFE, IVB
GLB WVRHB BTNXIGUVE.

- IHUE AVUFEUF ISXUGG

258.

PAEWUFSLY SG FRP HPO FL EYMLWH FRP
KLMAPY ALLB LV VBPPALQ.

- KPLBKP XUGRSYKFLY WUBNPB

259.

WIUS QJST FL KBTJW HFWY WYJW QFUE IR
LWARR. AD AUWFV JGTBFPJU YFLWIBS O,
YT YJE IUVS EIUT PIGGTBPFJVL.

- TWYJU LADVTT

260.

WND IZO'L TDL Z EHAHL NO ZOWLFHOR. LFV

ANBV WNDPBVZA, LFV XZBLFVB WND RVL.

- AHIFZVE TFVETJ

261.

EXPAK QDP QHDMAFL TUVHO. AB QDP BQH

DNAMABW BU BDJH THUTMH UXB UG

BQHEPHMRHP GUO D GHV QUXOP.

- HMBUF CUQF

262.

LI L JODGZD IOPB ZUD UDGOZ, RDGOTX

DWDOXZULRC NPOYM, LI IOPB ZUD UDGQ,

GTBPMZ RPZULRC.

- BGOJ JUGCGTT

263.

KB'W ALQP BU YJLB L EJQWUV MAU VJGJQ

TKGJW ZE. AJQUJW TJB QJCJCYJQJP, YZB

DJTJVPW VJGJQ PKJ.

- YLYJ QZBA

264.

BXOC XP CSZ HZOC BAOJE JD WBZKJEWD

SJOCXKL RWO BWYZ HL MZXMFZ RJCS DX

XMCJXDO.

- JOWWE HKXEV

265.

GSHC K LHX U VKXXVH WICHD K QAD QIINF,

UCM KZ UCD KF VHZX K QAD ZIIM UCM

EVIXSHF.

- MHFKMHYKAF HYUFWAF

266.

UQM UZ SRM PUES DMLHSJZHT

CHLTJSJME UZ SYHM ZYJMQNERJF JE SU

HQNMYESLQN LQN SU DM HQNMYESUUN.

- EMQMWL

267.

USFOF TC Y CTQPVF VTPSU XJ CDTFQDF,

YQW UX EOTPSUFQ TU YQMGSFOF TC UX

EOTPSUFQ TU FRFOMGSFOF.

- TCYYD YCTIXR

268.

HJFG IDWKJFD FBEDGNLRX ABDFR'G AB

ONKG QBJ YUKRRDA LG GB AB ABDFR'G

EDKR LG'F JFDUDFF.

- GNBEKF DALFBR

269.

SVI UNBY LPDLZB TCLD, TCLD DQYF YFI

IZIB,DFIV SVI WLVVSY TCLD DQYF L HIVWQP.

- ELPYFNB

270.

XFAJ VH EFZ FEXG HFLJZUVEW GFK SJJX,

VZ VH HFLJZUVEW GFK OF.

- OMAVO CVXQJTHFE

271.

AYVXV PXV SVD UERAPEZVR DYVE

PQVXUZPE YURAFXJ FSSVXR IR ADF ZBVPX

RUWVR FS P QFXPB BUEV.

- MFJ XVUW

272.

CWDSNBD EPNCGXFYX QKDWNP WJ BJXGXJJ
QPF EPNCGXFYX CWDSNBD QKDWNP WJ
MBDWGX.

- QRBR QEU

273.

LVFRN GVF JF TFL GYTL LF BHBLYLN
YTILVBTS WEFJAUN TFLVBTS.

- RYQKYJFE JYQB

274.

UGNH GL QHIHC NOGC, OQJ ZHCWOZL GB GL
O FXXJ BWGQF NXC KXLB XN EL BWOB GB GL
QXB.

- XLMOC DGUJH

275.

WA WE BUJI ZGRU AGRI HB ZLBUH AGCA
KCSGWURE LRKWUQ IBY GBZ FBZRLXYJ
AGRI CLR.

- SJWTR PCKRE

276.

W INTL DZ WF EGT PVDEG, PV X GDIT ZXNE
VO VDN XRTNWSXF GWPEVNB TADSXEWVF
NTQVCQTA XNVDFA EGT SWQWC LXN.

- XFPVF RVDFE

277.

QHFGTUFATG KVAQR LG NUHR FV LG U NVTF
VS RHNKHXQHMGR FGKYMHZAG SVT
UTVANHMP KGTFUHM GCVFHVMN.

- HTHN CATRVKY

278.

KW FWH VMWD DRUQ ZF XUIWCJQN SUCQ WX

QRNBUZN JL? QRN WSSWCQHMJQF QW

SGUF.

- ZJVN LJMBGNQUCF

279.

YVQ LQB FK WHY YVQ MFGG YH MFW.

QIQXBCHEB VUK YVUY. FY FK YVQ MFGG YH

OXQOUXQ YH MFW YVUY FKFJOHXYUWY.

- CHCCB LWFZVY

280.

D'NH WVBWOU UAHLQ GTMH QDGH BDQJ W

UGDVH TL GO XWRH QJWL LTQ, FPQ QJH

QJDLI DU, D ETL'Q BMDQH WFTPQ DQ.

- MTFHMQ UGDQJ

281.

VUTUHP AGAX JAVN TXUWA

YVHAXAONBQINBVR NFA NIONA UD NFA

IQAXBLIV KYTEBL.

- F. E QAVLWAV

282.

W CA CE CEZFJ-KCDPJFWK WE LBFWZWJE, C

KFCXXWKWXD WE FWDBLCDQLB CEH C

LJRCFWXD WE GJFWDWKX.

- D. X. BFWJD

283.

ZLA EGHJ OUVVAXAGYA NAZBAAG R MEEO

ORJ RGO R NRO ORJ UQ JECX RZZUZCOA.

- OAGGUQ Q. NXEBG

284.

B NPBCTUVY UM BAZBUI VA GVMUYQ.

KHKZWVYK KGMK UM BAZBUI VA SUYYUYQ.

- DUGGUK RKBY JUYQ

285.

LAPHYV ZNY Z BALFJHBZCYK BAJJHVHAR AI

JHCYNZCGNY, CTYZCNY, LGVHB ZRK ZJJ

CTY PHVGZJ ZNCV.

- WZTAA VYNHAGV

286.

NRW QTJVZFNBJM JO NJJ ICMS ZPWOZH

NRBMEP TWPZHNP BM NJJ ICMS ZPWHWPP

QWJQHW.

- GCTH ICTA

287.

V NE DEL QIWS OEHCKLISB. V QIWS FWOJ EQ LYIH.

-VBWWO WBVHEM

288.

GCJUBWD CGWBJUVF UA YGWPGVGS UM UC UA CUGS IL YUCJ SEFRWA CJWC YUDD VEC TGWX GZWRUVWCUEV.

- RWXFWXGC G. PVUFJC

289.

FPWNHPN NHZWPENF AEN CWHQ. UWANZVAKZN NHZWPENF AEN RNZFLHVUWAB.

- HWPLUVF SLCNI QVXWUV

290.

XRCFNWHAJ OXMWFW WVZF ZFK AV TNFXE

TMA VAGFNW AV TNFXE NFOVNRW.

- YHQQHXZ X. YXNR

291.

YLKEGOC YGDZ L WQGMOP GO DZM PLQE GU

VMDDMQ DZLO YLKEGOC LKBOM GO DZM

KGCZD.

- ZMKMO EMKKMQ

292.

XJBJO IGBJ MZ TX DTRJTXJ NAT GD AKBGXI

K LKF FKV. UTRTOOTN ETMSF LJ VTMOD.

- IGTBKXXGJ FJ DKFJSJJO

293.

TYB ABIJTY HPY KPEB P OXMMBIBYHB, PYO

BSBIDTYB JUTNQO VID.

- RTUY M. EBYYBOD

294.

PF HQKXQP, ZFE QXXV N SFFV

HBNSHQNPHFQ NQV N AHWX FU LEQY.

- PDFBNM XVHMFQ

295.

MVXCZCDPX TCZHCVX CR P JPBCXCPH

NIVSWG DGPHPDZNHCRZCD VJ PBNHCDPI

GCRZVHA.

- HVFNHZ EPXXNY

296.

YKUKPPKZ XJ MAZMGJ IPDJQ, ZXYQ SK

UXJYMRDJ XS XY GDY.

- A. U. UKSYTKUDPG

297.

FKO YLOTFOL DGGDLFPSVFZ OSTHEOQ UO

FD UTBO VUGDLFTSF QVMXDCOLVOM TSQ

VSCOSFVDSM.

- GKVEVG OUOTYITEV

298.

DWO EWTVD ERXXOEEOE DWUD XUJ QO

LUGJOM GJ U QVGOK DGAO UJM CGDWTRD

MGKKGXRZDN UVO JTD CTVDW ARXW.

- WOJVN KTVM

299.

G IFFT TGDF AYZVFOFB GL RFZUV GL RFZUV.

G IFFT TGDF VYGL GL ZTBFZKH ABGVVFU.

- TGT EZEH

300.

VZDB VR YPVQY XP YP GPFQ DR PQT PS XKT

YZTDXTRX ANCQGTZR VQ DETZVLDQ

KVRXPZI.

– RLPXX DQGTZRPQ

301.

FVK INTQOVFJ XV YTKKVM. FVK RK NEVW

INT. OKHQK KPVQV.

- SPVQIF OKQHIVM

302.

DIIJTXOKWNTREV LKOO XBJMR VJ YR D

UJSBERZ, EJV D ARWVKEDVKJE.

- ALKFNV A. RKWRENJLRB

303.

RFG YSQBRXPYRVSQ SA RFG PQVIGXBG VB

YGXREVQHK IGXK UPYF GEBVGX RS

GJTHEVQ RFEQ VB RFER SA RFG THEQR.

- CGSXC YFXVBRSTF

304.

JL LJN BNZDDK QZA Z YZO DHRN. JLS NGNJ Z

YZO OZK. MVAS YZO TLTNJSA.

- BNUHJZ YBNSS

305.

TVGKYNPNYF NA NWYGJJNUGWTG ZKPNWU XEW.

- KJCGVY GNWAYGNW

306.

D PQY'F EYQH HXKOK D'G UQDYU ZOQG XKOK, VMF D ROQGDTK DF HQY'F VK VQODYU.

- PNADP VQHDK

307.

RGNDGJ IPD PRE GJHJU ARBJ R AXECRFJ PRE GJHJU CUXJB RGNCPXGS GJI.

- RWMJUC JXGECJXG

308.

WLE IAJAMACYBAWK AD DTAXBAKP XEWS

DIAQKIQYKO BQITKWMWPH BW ETQBWEAI

YKO MABAPYBAWK.

- SYDWK IWWMQH

309.

MAYFVOMT QVPSUFR VP TUS   OKYMT.

- DYT NUITSMVT

310.

TAF KQA FGP RQXOGFAQO GU UKPA, VIP

GFDJ RQXOGFAQO GU PZAXQ GBF TXFLO.

- UQKFCDXF L. QGGOASADP

311.

PRTHPYTHUU WCCU FHWVLA LR PYXH. YL

DVLU W UDHGYWP FVMT RT UVTUHLU WTC

SWIHU TYEKL WYM USHPP FHLLHM.

- KHTMA MRPPYTU

312.

XRWNCUH XI Z UXF, Z AXXB CN Z SZT'N

AHNW IDCHTU. CTNCUH XI Z UXF, CW'N WXX

UZDB WX DHZU.

- FDXREPX SZDJ

313.

WIKUHUTX UM XIYIW CAI GWTRKIB. UC'M CAI

GITGKI LAT VMI UC CT HEUX GTLIW.

- FVKUEX PEMERKEXPEM

314.

EV BEKYIHKTIY HJ EV BRWY, GY HIY

HJKRVEJQYZ HK GQHK EJ XQRJYV SF

RKQYIJ.

-HVZIY NHTIREJ

315.

T FRKFXP CLRI IJFI UX OVLFILPI FPPLI KFP HGI

UX SJXPTWFR FQTRTIX, TI KFP UX ULHIFR

FQTRTIX.

- QVDWL MLHHLV

316.

UV BHE IHR'Y MLJS FHRVUISRFS, BHE'DD

LDNLBX VURI L NLB RHY YH NUR.

- FLCD DSNUX

317.

OQRK TKQTJK BMFE CE EQ SMTTKF, OQRK

BCOS CE BQLJW SMTTKF, QESKUO RMDK CE

SMTTKF.

- RCZSMKJ NQUWMF

318.

KIDL GH KGVL OB FIXERKOHH, QGUF UFL

FLOEU PGKKGBR XM OH UFL SEOGB

LWMUGLH.

- CXKLH ELBOEA

319.

KV KE IDVVDT VJ JZZDT RJ DUMYED VSHR

H IHA JRD.

-PDJTPD OHESKRPVJR

320.

TBVHA TNVMTW, TBVHA NQPYS, BSM DNJP

LDFNCPBSP, TBVHA BP WNVCJYTQ.

- RAYTJYB ABSMTYC

321.

IQ ZIV CE DVP NVWGYKQVWE QDVWKI PV

PYMQ GCEME ZCTT YNNVJHTCEI DVPICDK

CD TCRQ.

- JWIYJJYX YTC

322.

JWLPRLPKT YWGC W ILSC AS RYCLB AMP

RYWR HCBLGCT SBAO RYC JWLPRCB'T TAZI.

- GLPECPR GWP KAKY

323.

K'HR YAQYOX DRRB KBSRGRXSRJ KB SPR

JREGRXXKVB YX SPKX HRGO JGYLYSKT

EKHVSYA ERGKVJ KB YLRGKTYB PKXSVGO.

- GVB PVQYGJ

324.

ZQWEDAFADJ AK EUUHNAMX JHPQKWUS DH

TEVW TAKDEVWK. EQD AK VMHNAMX NBAZB

HMWK DH VWWR.

- KZHDD ECETK

325.

E PVZ'J NXZJ JV WO JFO ZODJ AEKFXOU

GVLPXZ, E VZUT NXZJ JV WO QVWO WLTXZJ.

- QVWO WLTXZJ

326.

GPGMC UVC RB OC XTBG, T'O SMCTWN SR

BTWU V IVC SR NGS LGSSGM.

- MVC XGITK

327.

S FBC'G JNYSNTN SC DXXSFNCGH. GUNEN

DEN BCYA NCXBICGNEH SC USHGBEA.

– QDJYB QSXDHHB

328.

DLW CBGJ DLABP MW LQIW DC KWQX AT

KWQX ADTWGK.

- KXQBEGAB Y. XCCTWIWGD

329.

CE C FJBS B WZZT BYS CH LBTJP LG VNZAJ

WZSG PZ MZAS YZ ECFJ MBY JDJF VBFL LJ,

C TYZV HNBH CP UZJHFG.

- JLCAG SCMTCYPZY

330.

HNJBJ LNJ DKGBGL YZJD TZL HZBA HGLN

LNJ NITY, LNJBJ GD TZ IBL.

- XJZTIBYZ YI OGTEG

331.

FOS EWSCF NKFO JX JAW FLNSG LG FOCF

FSVORJDJEK LG VJNNARLVCFLJR.

- DLMMK DCWGSR

332.

XPIW HPCSX, XPIW HPCSX. EXWM BUJ XPIW

MUSXCMF WTKW XPIW HPCSX.

- HZPMDCMW ZCIWZK

333.

YJV LXVKY WGVKQ WB YXEYJ DKR KDD

EQOTCGWIVXVO ZVBWXV HV.

- TCKKG QVPYWQ

334.

RPFNDHAHDS HO DNLHBC DVF MFOD

OLHQQO NBT DFRVBHXYFO JPIU FWKFPDO

NPIYBT SIY NBT HUKPIAHBC YKIB DVFU.

- YBLBIGB

335.

TS T'U PMOOR BVJJ R QVRJ XBMQE, T'U

PMOOR XBRQB CTBN UE ORUV.

- FVOZQTKF JRURQ

336.

XE VWC VXIC RS BTLHCFV BCSCTV,

ZXQVRLG ITG YC ECTLCFV.

- NXPPXTI IQHXEPCG

337.

MW MD GFFXR KX, ZES TMYY EDANXBV EYY

BMR YMZJR JKD DBF XKRB-JKDDNS

WMSPFA.

- WAESG YYNVO TAMPBD

338.

TIVJSLX KDSLXP RVHAP KDAR PAAR RUIA

IAVW VLT RVHAP RA QAAW RUIA VWSZA.

- TVZST XALKWARVL

339.

TPJVB DUBJPVBAPJ UQ QUCGDE DVITAVTJ

YLVPTJX KUBL CJVIUIT BW BLJ ABCWQB

GWQQUZDJ XJTPJJ.

- JOPV GWAIX

340.

QZ YZF ELGK DZL IGOK MXNIO, ELGK FZ UI

OFLZYJIL VIY.

- RZAY D. CIYYIQK

341.

H'E GXV GN QAV EGFQ AZEJUV DVGDUV

BGZ'UU DMGJLJUB VOVM EVVQ.

- FRH ELFR QAV FUZED PGK

342.

FNI QC GBI F TFGJQLNFZI; QI QC ITH

INFGCWQCCQBG BZ ZHHKQGA ITH FNIQCI

TFC HOVHNQHGLHJ.

- KHB IBKCIBM

343.

EU MJA VJ KQOR MJA IJDW, MJA'II BWDWC

KJCZ O VOM EB MJAC IEUW.

- HOCN OBRQJBM

344.

XUFD C UDO JDFNUXAXIV TXAAH XYDT VXK,

RZ VXK'TD UXJ QCTJ XZ JND HJDCWTXAADT,

VXK'TD QCTJ XZ JND TXCP.

- HJDOCTJ STCUP

345.

GU DJ BUUA, OFA GU AU BUUA, RM OVV SJ

NOQJ GU AU.

- TUNF OAOEM

346.

DOC JRO PSXI LDGZRHC JRYCA R

JRKDZSXU.

-ROWZCP KRLYADO

347.

EM EGWJDGD ZEMMCG UFM ARGW VCMDQ

RM WRN BCZHDGN. WD VFNG UFM ARGW

WCBD RM WRN WDEUG EML LUDEVN RM

WRN WDEL.

- DVRJ P

348.

CRPGCJP JR JDN IRMAJOP GCXGPB.

CRPGCJP JR JDN FRTNOAZNAJ XDNA VJ

UNBNOTNB VJ.

– ZGOW JXGVA

349.

QPM FYWM YU QPM QMDJPMF GZ QY JFMDQM

QPM JYACGQGYAZ UYF GATMAQGYA

FDQPMF QPDA BFYTGCM FMDCN-IDCM

HAYKWMCLM.

- ZMNIYSF B

350.

U DGHX QB AH XUGSDGQHX. TBN U QML QB

AH PYDGHX.

- HOZUG WBGQHOOB

351.

MXDMZDQS DV ZFL EYMSRF QB

LSHDSLLYDSH ZFMZ DV ILMVZ BQYHDXDSH

QB KDVZMPLV.

– BYLLKMS UGVQS

352.

HFK KGGKOAK MN HEYK NELKOJGFLR LG HM
PIUK ICCMBIOAK NME IOMHFKE'G CLHHCK
CIRGKG.

– JIZLJ GHMEKW

353.

SJZB HIE SJTT AHG OSJPHPTR WUQFI KJSF
YAHI UY'G YHBFI.

- ZAHSTUF LHYYG

354.

LMD LMYTOF Y ZHTL LC UTCZ HWD YT
QCCUF. XG QDFL KWYDTI YF LMD XHT
ZMC'JJ ODL XD H QCCU YHYT'L WDHI.

- HQWHMHX JYTSCJT

355.

GPAHA VHA GPHAA YVJGPYZD YHJALTU, VL

FDT EJYA, VL FDT TFO, VLT HAVTR IFLAR.

– WALBVIJL YHVLNDJL

356.

RKOEFBJ FU DFIT WOIFBJ OB TYXKTUUFZT

JTUHQKT, EFHM HMT ORZOBHOJT NL

XTKWOBTBAT.

- MTBKF WOHFUUT

357.

OCNK RHO KHGCRXPXVA FXHU LU GTHNKH

RHO XYYXTKBRLKLHU KX FX N MXW KCNK

GBUKXIHTU ONRK FXRH.

- KLI X'THLPPA

358.

R OYSSCW VKMPYURJV WPV RKMCGWYSOV

CZ Y NCCQ WVYOPVG.

- WVKMTV NGYSQRS

359.

Z HSXT ASRTDB RM MCITCDT EJC RM HJTST

ACS UCX EJTD JT'B SZHJTS GT ZDUEJTST

TYMT.

– YTD ETRD

360.

BR GHRZT FJZBZFZXW XGE LRBQZLO, TR

LRBQZLO,IM LRBQZLO.

- GJZXBRBVM

361.

KDFUDGKND KW GVU GIOUDG NR BNCGV, IW

ECXLZUDG KW NR ILU.

- ENDIGVID WJKRG

362.

J NBVYHAE WE BLBWJBV PQBL J WTMB YQBW

WE GHJBLNV.

- TKHTQTW DJLFADL

363.

TY PHYHVTDWI LIAITS XG DISSIV SPTY T

LXGPHYHVTDWI KXRSHVB.

- UXWWTVL AXWWUHVI

364.

MS PZSKMN SE UFDJJEKJ DMAVMNDSM IPM

TVWJPIV NRV VUUVMNDPJ VJVZVMN SE

DZPBDMPNDSM.

- VLGPTL RSWWVT

365.

FANT AH IZMKC SX LYVFAEK, GMI HZ YVT

XZM.

- HITDCYEAT GTEETII CTEVX

366.

LEYM KEZMJQPBZS RAOMP UBMJ LBM

PZCMJRM VMLUMMJ LUA SMASCM ZP

RAOKAELWVCM.

– QWDZQ LNPAJ TMJLEN

367.

TGEJ IGFHS MQEXUQ WYQ IGFHS

VGZDSXWHGD GD AYHEY H TQMZHFW UN

FHVQ.

- O.J. TGAFHDB

368.

RMX AXH QIUBXNQXIR RL EIH AQIN LW

MEJJQIXYY LB YCZZXYY QY RL IXDXB UQDX

KXYY RMEI HLCB GXYR.

- BCYYXKK YQTTLIY

369.

FOKOY UOQ GTEY POSW PSFZ WTNF. FOKOY

ZCKO EX SFW JCQ WTNF SFW ZYCOKO.

LCFW SFTQPOY NSG.

- JSQAPOU XSCZO

370.

UPT XTHGVQVUZSD SK ZDXTRTDXTDHT ZJ

V JVHQTX RVQU SK VFTQZHVD PZJUSQN.

- RVWG LZGGFSQ

371.

NTAX YKTYWK CTSWZ IDXPKI JK VKIXDQG

XPKL'IK NQAKIDJWK, XPDG IQAR JKQGB

PDYYL.

- ITJKIX DGXPTGL

372.

QEJH PZ OPQ MWE CZZ BPZ FELFCFUJZ MWE

VQ BPZ FSGQCCFUJZ.

- TXWEA J. RWFEZC

373.

FMGJMGP FQQWMG WMGZNZ SY ZDOPF OR

1928 LSZ QRM QI PFM VOGPOMZP

MYMBPOQRZ OR SDMGOBSR FOZPQGT.

- HQZMCF BNDDORZ

374.

IRAG KNO RNK HDDAMANXXO ELJMRCK

CWCQO RHXC AJ RCQ MQNBO IAMYCI.

- YATPCQXO YAJMNAK

375.

KYI NYX'M PXYV VELM KYI ULX SAWW

CTRYDT KYI MDK.

- RDLXPQAX FATDUT

376.

OUZHCWQU ZGHFO FG RGU EHVJ

OVCKKSTK FZCXJZO.

- IHTKH AGJKQG

377.

KUHJONHLOJ UC CHOJDB DUHP HPJ

DOJXENVJ QS YJB DPQ PNAJ YUBTJT

FJZQBT OJNCQB HPJ QGUBUQBC QS

QHPJOC.

- AUOVUBUN DQQKS

378.

FZ PWZV ZHZJOSFAWI XMCLS DASZJXSLJZ

ZBEZNS FCV SC ZWQCO AS.

- QCKZNF FZDDZJ

CRYPTOGRAMS

379.

OX NXKMXZNTX EOW ZT COBM WMXWM NX

ZEM QTVAR NZ LNXNWEMW NX, XTZ NX ZEM

QTVAR NZ WZOVZMR.

- ZNC T'VMNAAP

380.

DZ CZHUZPBM CT TCJGFX D KUFFBY YWB

LBUTZ'P PDIU WCT ULSVDPCBZ PBB

TUMCBSTFX.

– VWDMFUT IUPPUMCZE

381.

VKWCMPWYMC VCS FC WZ JMCCSZF, EZW

WDC ZWDCM HPU MZYES.

- KIFPKV TPSPMC

382.

W OUDWOTD, W FQODTWOKTD, WV

WTOQMOQZ DSATDMMQPV OUWO EPDM VPO

MADWI XPT QOM PYV OQND UWM VP

TDFDRWVZD.

- EWTQP XP

383.

S BTSXY BTD FQBRHFBSRX RJ ZSGSRX SG F

HQVT MSKKDU NDFW BTFX BTD SXZDXBSRX

RJ LDUGLDVBSZD.

- BUDZRU LFKWDX

384.

BTI FGD HU SMU VTTD GDC KSJYY HU

AUGYTIK TP SMU KSGOK.

- QGOB GYYGD

385.

ZKYYSJDAA MQTBA KN TXQ TBJ USQDASLDA,
KJL SA JTN NT GD YSPEDL SJ ANQKJMDQ'A
MKQLDJA.

- LTXMVKA FDQQTVL

386.

GBX'CO DRO BAO IRB ZT IOPN. GBX IZVV
AOLOC NABI VBLO BC KCZOASTRZQ. PAS
Z KOOV TBCCG KBC GBX.

- F. N. CBIVZAW

387.

JUGHG RW YTQS YTG BGHWYT AUY KYOQN
GCGH VIMG SYO UIBBS, ITN JUIJ BGHWYT
RW SYO.

- NICRN ZOHTW

388.

XEV YLGYMKNXLQT QB YQTBLZVTYV LW

OVXXVG XENT XEV YLGYMKNXLQT QB

IQTVA.

- PNIVW INZLWQT

389.

MGUCFGC VLX MCK WUVUKM KB

RFBSWCJTC, EAK MPBAWJ FBK MCK

WUVUKM KB UVLTUFLKUBF.

- ECOKOLFJ OAMMCWW

390.

QBJYFQ, FC KFLSWB, JTW YZB VQRBQYFS

FC AVCCBSBQYVTI KTIKLILW WF ZVW MITKB

VQ YZB YTIB VW ELVYB WMBKVTI.

- HVY JVIIVTDW

391.

ZSD YWEJJ IEKZ QH OPLQKELMD ZSEZ VD

EKKELPD ELA MJEYYOHR VD POBD ZSD

LEWD QH GLQVJDAPD.

- EWNKQYD NODKMD

392.

LGEZP CQUPKVRSUH CNQ YSGA ASPQP UR

UK UA, KNA CNQ YSGA DGK TP WNAAPK

NZA NC UA.

- S. DEGM AQZITZEE

393.

B QPK'M UHKM H GFHJI SBDMPEC TPKMS.

GFHJI SBDMPEC BD HTVEBJHK SBDMPEC.

- TPEAHK YEVVTHK

394.

EAVJ UEF YDRFKJ EFX CMOX KJBGJVX

XOBXJB SDHJ, DX XOBXJB WJXXJK XMOA

OXXJAXDEA. WFX UEF MOZJ XE RJX XMJKJ.

- GDAH

395.

KIMWWOVUOJ LMFO WPCO PVDOYOJDPVU,

INGOHOY NHOYKNLPVU DIOL PJ GIMD

LMFOJ WPCO LOMVPVUCEW.

- LMYF DGMPV

396.

AWJ TDMC EMKBJ OHBBJOO BTYJO VJPTXJ

ZTXU RORD AWJ IRBARTDKXC.

- NRDBJ MTYVKXIR

397.

TIC'B BZKLHBLC EL XGBZ DIOL, AHAS.

DLB'P NRPBQI XHDJGCQ GC BZL KHGC.

- AGDDGL ZIDGTHS

398.

RBMYM'Q FZQR QIHM HNUXA XG RYZRB NGK

BIGMQRP NGK ICMGGMQQ.

- LYNGW IAMNG

399.

OTFE VMC GFF B UMMR WMXF, DMMH ZMA B

KFSSFA MEF.

- FWBECFD DBGHFA

400.

NMTCVMC DVQ WCMAVYXYBF DIC LADW LC

MDV QY. EYIDXTWF TN LADW LC DBICC LC

NAYGXQ YI NAYGXQ VYW QY.

- C. Y. LTXNYV

401.

EFA VXXNP EFTE EFA LXOCS BTCCP

GKKXOTC TOA VXXNP EFTE PFXL EFA LXOCS

GEP XLH PFTKA.

- XPBTO LGCSA

402.

TSSB LQMZRBI YQZ EMFZ ICYQI. DSK BSR'C

YEXYDI IZZ CUZW, HKC DSK FRSX CUZD YQZ

YEXYDI CUZQZ.

- VSRLKVMKI

403.

SNP UQSRVT KRTNSO YLS QD 1965 CKQJTNS

YV PVX SQ SNP JTMI ARW LKQF HPKRQX RV

YWPKRLYV NROSQKI.

- MROY WJKZQFOZR

404.

NAMMH OR SZB OGSBMBRS FUOL DH SZARB

NZA DAMMAN SMAYDTB.

- CBAMCB NURZOGCSAG

405.

UEHRBIBP QSZ HPB, XB H FSSN STB.

- HXPHEHK YATVSYT

406.

ZT VQ LKGGP, NQ WODZ ETZ VQ ZTT

YTEYQJEQM NAZLTZLQJD.

- KRVQJZ YKWOD

407.

W AJLS RF NLZQ EFFYR OMJZ W OLR L

YWS IMLI W SWSZ'I JXJZ YZFO OJAJ

RMLVWZD NJ HV.

- RIFANTQ

408.

FTK WDZE SDHYF MGSM, HPB BDP'K FKDC

KGYY WDZ STK KMTET.

- RD VHQOFDP

409.

E'F GTZDDK DIIREAU SIGBZGH JI LTTEAU

BQZJ DEST CGEAUL JI FT.

- GEQZAAZ

410.

ZXEXYQ VZXRX PK VDW VJ UGW MEWXUWKU

LVBPUPYPXDK PD XRWEPYXD GPKUVEH.

- IVGD LVFGVEWUT

411.

FHPTHLOBWU BD WRM SJBNML HT TLMMCHO

JPC WRM MPMOU HT ILHQWR.

- SHRP T. XMPPMCU

412.

TJX'DD EGUGF SCEH WGQIG JS LCEH XEKCD

TJX DCNKGE KJ TJXF MGQFK.

- RGJFRG LCIMQGD

413.

MTB RNV'U IZEA BJ ZV PZKA. MTB CBGU

RNV'U XT ZU, VT WNUUAY HQNU ZU ZG

UQNU ZG ITZVI TV

-.CTAM CTYXZGTV

414.

K BACZXV SICYVUBKNAIC KSUIBB NLV

NKQXV RANL K RABV HKC AB QVNNVU NLKC

NVC JVKUB HVUV BNGPJ IT QIIFB.

- LVCUJ XICZTVXXIR

415.

KBF AFUVKMRVI KBMYO UAWVK IFUTYMYO

MG YWAWPJ DUY KUEF MK UZUJ RTWS

JWV.

- A. A. EMYO

416.

GF GWDNQD SEQD BGMV BNQ SVGQEWNFC

DAAPQ FAD NF DBV BGFO, IED NF DBV VTV.

- SNUBVPGFCVPA

417.

HWYDZUO YB ZBG VLGB ZG UTB DFYB QTMW

LQLG GLL VMB DFYB TMW NZUH

MUHLWGBYUHG.

- NZEEYWH GFLLBG

418.

FRX'UI SRL LKI CXD, FRX'UI SRL LKI GRRD, NDV FRX'UI SRL LKI ARTTODS CLRDIC.

- HIOLK AOQKNAVC

419.

GA GX XANFCBW EJZ JCW SWWKX INFZC SJNZFNI ZGAEJYA LCJZGCB FA SGNXA ZEWNW JCW GX BJGCB.

- BYXAFO QFEKWN

420.

HAX ORIX HT WAYXAFWHA. QXTHOX ZHR VBA WAYXAF WF, ZHR UBYX FH WDBLWAX WF.

- NBDXC LRAA

421.

SP XIIWIRQHB CXYH KCXLFHQ, JRI

BMSHJMQP DMRAQ CXYH IM NHXQ XAA SP

JMMOB IM TWLQ MRI CMD ICHP CXYH.

- WNDWL BCXD

422.

TBNE ABYVN HKQ HJBLE HN IHDDG HN EIQG

THVQ LD EIQCK TCWXN EB JQ.

- HJKHIHT YCWMBYW

423.

XM LMB OQHV GWCBHAQC. UMZ DWPP ALMD

OHWPZVQ. KMLBWLZQ BM VQHKS MZB.

- EQLTHGWL OVHLAPWL

424.

QPJ VPS'W YBUF WP XJMS XPPNL WP

VFLWMPQ B IJKWJMF. ZJLW TFW CFPCKF

WP LWPC MFBVHST WYFA.

- MBQ XMBVXJMQ

425.

F YCRFYCY KAMN ENA MCWCL QA IEKB FM

EMZAMC'D DSEYAI. FP F PEFK, AL FP F

DXRRCCY EQ KCEDQ F YFY ED F OCKFCWC.

- ISFQMCZ S

426.

XW RJDMD'Y NVD RJXVL X'P LNNT QR, XR'Y

LQRJDMXVL IDNIBD RNLDRJDM RN TN

YNPDRJXVL WGV.

- TQZD LMNJB

427.

GB FWW MJN MJHIPR H'LN WGRM, H EHRR

EO EHIX MJN EGRM.

- GUUO GRCGQDIN

428.

EOIYI PD BV LVVZ ZXR VY GXZ ZXR, VBCR

LVVZ VY GXZ XSEPVBD.

- XNPE FXCXBEYP

429.

DQRAFQA NRTAD OD IFMZWAUNA, JOX

MFWG BPRWMDMBPG QSF NRTA OD

ZRDUMY.

- ZRWW UOCSFX

430.

TA'G WUA ACEA LZ OGZ AZICWUVUHJ, LZ

VTRZ AZICWUVUHJ.

- HUKXBZJ BZHHTU

431.

NZD KIAFJ MSGCM. KD MNVWQFD IC. GN GM

DCIVPZ.

- TIFVW WTTBCC

432.

RGYVY NVY QGWVZP AH RGY GYNVRP WC

RGY XWPR VYQUTYPP EGAQG QNHHWR OY

RWIQGYZ EARGWIR YXWRAWH.

- YZKNV NTTYH DWY

433.

NYNMPZAVFD VW AGMS RNXTMN VZ VW

NGWP.

-ITAGFF UTOXDGFD YTF DTNZAN

434.

EQC AWMKUQMXUK WO Q BHUT HB

MUKQOHG.

– FHOKLV EUHCODJ

435.

T'D L ZTFWVPA OMQQ, FV T'UK OKKI

PKLYTIE JVWF VQ OVVCF VI TPTFZ LIY

LDKPTGLI ZTFWVPA.

- FZKLDMF

436.

RCD NVGGDNR VNKDWR PJ HFJD IPQ FN
RCVR NWFDIWD AVRCDUN MIPQHDGAD
JVNRDU RCVI NPWFDRS AVRCDUN
QFNGPT.

- FNVVW VNFTPO

437.

CL'I DOHPL GDACRM EWTIHRDJCLB. CL'I
RHL DOHPL OWCRM LGW ODU MPB, CL'I
DOHPL WRLWTLDCRCRM EWHEJW.

- ZJHBU SDBKWDLGWT

438.

HLPSZEPKZS LF PWS EZP QB DZLPLRM

FQVSPWLRM PWEP DLHH JS ZSEG PDLXS.

CQKZREHLFV DWEP DLHH JS MZEFUSG EP

QRXS.

- XIZLH X

439.

TQSX JQZVTL, TCSX RXIXDCYJTL, WUDX

HXXVTL, JVXUE EQIHTL, TXUSX BAX DXJB

BC RCH.

- DCIUTH DXURUI

440.

NQCG MRS UCUMSTCF MRKNCTIQ MRS

HSCYUF, TK TF KQCG KQYK NC LCZMUC

MEH.

- LTEE ZETGKMG

441.

GT KIJWVY'U RTWPTQT PU FLD IYWC

FTVYTDVLC. LYV PU FLD ALVT FIHDT FGTY

GT HTLWPMTV PU FLD LKUJLWWC UJTDVLC.

- UE SWJYT

442.

TKBJKBC CNNJ XZGDPOI KI PGID. CPVVKBC

VYPF VN XZGD GI G VPGF KI GBNVYPO

IVNOD.

- SGIPD IVPBCPZ

443.

UNP CGWF TQF UC NQMP Q YJEPGB ED UC VP

CGP.

-JQWON TQWBC PSPJDCG

444.

CMGMT AHU BDD HCUSZ UBOBTTBL LPFU

XBH JFC RB UBRFX.

- UPBOFE NMDDMTEBC

445.

VCZJGK CVB QRRLM QKNRVW ZR ZIK KTKM

ZICZ MKK ZIKA.

- GCNYI DCNBR KAKGMRV

446.

SE YPQQXJM SN MQKBX, MTVY TVQA QAX

UHJJXEQ,SE YPQQXJM SN OJVEUVOBX,

MQPEW BVCX P JSUC.

- QASYPM ZXNNXJMSE

447.

F MDXN DBINDLZ RNOOBNL FO GCI QZRNBG

RC GBDOONIZ DVL WIFOFWFRQ JC LCUV

OMN RDQN LIDFV DVL F DQ TEFON GINN.

- JNCIJFD C

448.

SBRL WBXL CQ BOO VCZX HLHCXFLK. QCX

VCZ WBYYCS XLOFIL SULH.

- ACA MVOBY

449.

E CRYI RP EYS CTVZT KVK HRS MGFVH VH

GARSVRH VN HRS EYS.

- LEQX ZGBEHHG

450.

Z LNQOTK RDT UZQNO ZVTPG GDN NZQGD

RCSS QNOTKZGN RCGD CGO LPQCGI.

- OZSSI YTB

451.

E'T CWJ YC ECNQCJWX. E MKIJ FYCJ JW

TYGQ JBECZI RQJJQX.

- LYCEQU QG

452.

MBZBE NTMLCPB FYB PGUB TL OTCE

XWONYBNH DGFY FYB PGUB TL OTCE

FWRBMF.

- QWERTM AEWMJT

453.

IZCGKZG FKL TCNGSFNHSG FSG KJN NBJ

NDCKUI, WHN NBJ ICLGI JV JKG NDCKU.

- NDJOFI DHETGR

454.

QRX TGQCWQ AVWQ QGTCD DBQ BDME RCW

XEX PVQ TMWB RCW WBVM.

- UTWWCME NTDZCDWNE

455.

CPJLBOJSBL PI JVL ESLIJPDA KPASI JVL

OAIZLB.

- BDCOAH QOBJVLI

456.

Z HGAWNE VZGGJKB CPBH. YKYAGJKB

SZBH XAGKFKG.

- YZGE SAP GKHHAO

457.

BS IXK'HA OJQVBGU TXOG CNA HBUNC DJCN

JGT IXK'HA OBQQBGU CX VAAD OJQVBGU,

AFAGCKJQQI IXK'QQ PJVA DHXUHAYY.

- LJHJWV XLJPJ

458.

KST HOBBTUTYIT XTKQTTY WTYOVN EYH

NKVLOHOKP ON, WTYOVN SEN OKN

GOCOKN.

- EGXTUK TOYNKTOY

459.

TCXNZXZ TCU LMZX OINRQCUB HIY CUDMZU

XY WMX QYHB XIUNC OCTKYBZ.

- TR INCZOIDURQ

460.

WCI JFNXNAZ AW LIYJAY RJP WCAIYJLRYS

WCI JFNXNAZ AW CPY QNPYXZ ARY

TIWSCLAP WD WCI NHBYHANWH.

- QRNAHYZ O. ZWCHU

461.

TYIQN RTXKBF T RKLITXQ DN LZYYQNKBF T

RKLYDNIZBQ, IAQ RTB DY FQBKZL TGUTEL

FQIL HTMX DB AKL YQQI.

- BTJDGQDB HDBTJTNIQ

462.

JXFICQZQLB GE DXEJ OIXC GJ DHGCLE

YXQYZX JQLXJIXH.

- KRJJ KMZZXCOXL

463.

RBATBSRBH RL Y LDRVV SJYS LXPT

ZTXZVT JYAT YBE LXPT ZTXZVT EXB'S. NGS

WXG QYB VTYUB JXO SX RBATBS.

- UYW EXVNW

464.

OXGYBXY PGBHO XWEYO NSEY YTOGVL

JRTB TBOUYEO.

-FYTB ESOJTBH

465.

X BMRP PQ WQ KQBR XR PCY CXVPQJS

UQQAV BXPC BCMP X'LY MGCXYLYK.

- EMRKQ RQJJXV

466.

YCV ZB EQUC VI UCQE, VGTFP, BACQP QFE

DUTVC.

- NIGF QEQSB

467.

PKH LHXGLW BZL XZLV XHTT WZMH RN PKH

ZDDZLPCMRPO PZ WZ AZLH.

- FZMGN NGTV

468.

YEM EQGSMG YEM JWBVTKJY, YEM

UGMQYMG YEM YGKHPXE.

- UMWGUM RQLEKBUYWB

469.

BE RDB CU KEEJ QBEAKG NE KEFQVB

DBENGQV RDB TCNGEAN GCU LEBUQBN.

- DOVDGDR YCBLEYB

470.

LJB'S NGS EJKI QPZZOBGHH LGZGBL JB

HJVGSQOBT EJK VPE NJHG.

- R.H. NGFOH

471.

ISM BMGHTDM EC HTIMUXIVUM TDBTGXIMQ

ISM BMGHTDM EC X DXITED.

- NESXDD ZEHCPXDP RED PEMISM

472.

HUKK HCU HVLHC, MTVP CNVE NIE FTYU HT

EXIIUV TI HXYU.

- DUVNKE OTVE

473.

QMWXRQ WXML XIUMLVPVLY WRZXLCTCYB,

UCKRQL UML GQRSRQE WC WRZXLVSB UML.

- LVZCTME YCURP KMOVTM

474.

SPKOCWH CI WFR OVKR FWM IMMI, NXR

OVKR FWM GKWJKLM FRVMPI IMM.

- MSHKP SMHKI

475.

TXH ZDYYBMBAXQCH TJSTXMAJ

QAMRXLCLFH BZ BXJBZQBXFDBZRTUCA

YVLG GTFBM.

- TVQRDV MCTVPA

476.

CSRLFP RFF DSC ORC GBRCQ RQJSLGABP,

VIB AZ PNI XRCB BN BSGB R DRC'G

OMRLROBSL, YAJS MAD HNXSL.

- RVLRMRD FACONFC

477.

BT QOGQCO GUCP SUOD KGD KMAV B DGAS

ZG JMBU FPFMEZOAP. BZ DGNCVU'Z EOOF

EG DGUVOATNC MZ MCC.

- FBLKOCMUJOCG

478.

HF HN WKMR FS VKHC, AIF HF HN ESMNB

YBDBM FS WKDB FMHBR FS NIPPBBR.

- FWBSRSMB MSSNBDBCF

479.

DBOBZ LIKJE ERSE XIK HSD HRSDCB

RQNEIZX. XIK SMZBSLX RSOB.

- ASZCB FQBZHX

480.

XGRGCF NYLOOF ELNYP JZ FGW'NY

SJPYNLROY, PG FGW SJUAV LP KYOO RY

ALTTF.

- EFXVAJL XYOSP

481.

ALVNX TUV'P ZMX XLM CUGGJVNDD, ZMP

JP TUV ZMX XLM U XUTCP ZJQ NVLMQC PL

GMOO MG EJQCP UOLVQDJSN JP.

- SURJS ONN ELPC

482.

POB FD AOXOXLOA - TQO LTTI, TQO EOQ,

TQO RZUPM, WQM TQO BOWRZOA RWQ

RZWQYO BZO KTAPM.

- XWPWPW NTFDWGVWU

483.

KHXHD WMMR SZLR IKWHJJ NMI ZDH

AWZKKFKY GM YM GEZG UZN.

- EHKDN CZXFC GEMDHZI

484.

NPNST AWT MU W XND AWT, WXA TZB'YY

XNPNS JN WJYN VZ RMXA QWLLMXNUU MR

TZB AZX'V KZPN ZX.

-GWSSMN BXANSDZZA

485.

M HSJX XD XSTXQ SJL UZDAO MJ QSVI LSO,

SJL JQRQA WQ SNASML XD QCGQAMQJVQ

GSMJ.

- TOZRMS GZSXI

486.

VIM BYVMDDBZMYV OHM JP HRBMYRM GYU

VMRIYJDJZA GTM VIM VJJDH XBVI XIBRI VJ

GRIBMNM G YMX UBTMRVBJY.

- QGRSOM PTMHRJ

487.

UJWK OJ AJCLJMUP RJUQI TUQ MU VUPPUQ,

OJB LCLPK FOJ AI UP ITUHWB VL OJ

AJCLJMUP.

- POWXT QOWBU LFLPIUJ

488.

CSBWP YAXRDGL AX VBGR DJ BKIGAWBF YAXRDGL, BFT AR XYDHST CI RGIBRIT BX XHWY.

- ZBFISSI KDFBI

489.

IGVMFVMK VD DPEW AVDYRQPSZ. PQPSZ KRRA GSFVDF IGVMFD JUGF UP VD.

- CGYHDRM IREERYH

490.

ZCL KVWLCB WC U GWKLIWYL WQ YMAS, IRZ UVL YUCO,ISVLL UVL SUVBGO TZQQWEGL.

- SLCVO UBUYQ

491.

VLQ QFFQAIQ KN VQILAKHKEO CF GO AK

ZQRAF RAOVLCAE VQILAKHKECIRH.

- ZRJVCA LQCSQEEQJ

492.

LHZDJ QYD WBD YDQX QYABVWDAWC HT

CHAVDWR.

- ABDY

493.

EPUH YEMPCHRWH HFYWL YU HP HCN RWB

YWUMYCQ MQPMJQ UP HFRH HFQN TRW KQ

LCQRH YW ZFRHQGQC HFQN ZRWH HP BP.

- OPKQ KCNRWH

494.

XKO RWMWXTJ AOEGJHXWGL WQ PTA DGAO
QWMLWPWNTLX XKTL XKO WLEOLXWGL GP
BAWXWLM GA OEOL GP ZAWLXWLM.

- RGHMJTQ OLMOJSTAX

495.

RBDDAKIGG CTIG KTV XTKGAGV AK
DBGVAUIG BKC BULGIUIKVG OLV AK
ZAEVLTLG BXVAZAVAIG.

-BEAGVTVMI

496.

SX TED BLR BXLBSF EX XBSYDLR TED FEQ'J
FRHRLCR JE GR HDNNRHHXDY.

- NIBLYRH GBLVYRT

497.

CVA VYFFTIAKK NB GNHU DTBA QAFAIQK
HFNI CVA JHYDTCG NB GNHU CVNHLVCK.
CVAUABNUA, LHYUQ YPPNUQTILDG.

- XYUPHK YHUADTHK

498.

YV NPCRATX'S SVMGP WLVMS HCCIN. YV
NPCRAT SVMGP M ACDV CB LVMTEXW.

- H. B. NIEXXVL

499.

QFU'W GFEEC RSFJW SIBUO R YWRE, GFEEC
RSFJW QFBUO OFFQ GFEZ, RUQ RMM WDRW
GBMM TFPI WF CFJ.

- BTI TJSI

500.

DSYQMOY GVUUSMJ KMO NMJ'Y QVFA
AJAPIK, DSYQMOY AJAPIK KMO QVFA
JMYQSJI.

- NMJVWN YPOBG

HINTS

1: T=N, I=E	2: L=O, A=S	3: R=A, O=D
4: N=T, C=F	5: V=N, P=R	6: B=T, W=A
7: B=I, L=Y	8: V=E, F=S	9: Y=E, S=T
10: V=E, W=H	11: B=E, I=F	12: H=E, F=A
13: Y=O, S=U	14: A=T, J=M	15: I=N, J=Y
16: V=E, B=W	17: I=O, W=H	18: W=A, X=I
19: N=S, V=R	20: G=S, J=P	21: T=R, L=S
22: M=T, H=R	23: C=E, U=G	24: J=O, I=S
25: B=I, Q=K	26: T=O, E=A	27: H=E, R=S
28: Z=E, I=R	29: U=O, Y=D	30: R=E, A=O
31: Y=N, P=L	32: W=T, N=L	33: Z=N, M=D
34: B=E, X=O	35: U=A, A=T	36: I=A, O=E
37: I=E, K=S	38: H=I, G=P	39: W=E, H=R
40: K=O, P=A	41: F=R, D=W	42: X=I, L=H
43: L=N, Z=A	44: G=O, W=A	45: K=T, L=O
46: O=N, S=B	47: N=I, W=F	48: Y=E, W=L
49: O=R, V=C	50: S=H, W=I	51: M=I, R=C
52: K=I, B=J	53: Y=A, F=O	54: H=N, R=F
55: K=A, V=D	56: W=T, O=E	57: R=E, Q=S
58: R=E, F=M	59: F=N, S=E	60: Z=H, K=R
61: Q=I, J=O	62: X=S, Y=V	63: J=E, V=G
64: J=E, N=B	65: C=N, K=A	66: W=R, S=I

67: Y=A, Z=T	68: T=S, P=D	69: T=E, L=A
70: R=S, P=K	71: J=O, X=T	72: I=S, R=T
73: M=E, P=J	74: P=I, K=H	75: C=H, L=P
76: V=A, Z=M	77: Y=O, Q=B	78: G=A, N=I
79: F=O, A=Y	80: J=E, B=T	81: D=N, T=L
82: F=E, H=S	83: C=I, V=L	84: B=I, R=N
85: Q=I, P=D	86: X=E, B=R	87: X=O, U=K
88: C=N, L=J	89: Z=R, K=S	90: L=A, J=S
91: K=S, N=H	92: B=E, L=H	93: T=A, H=R
94: F=E, R=O	95: P=E, I=N	96: F=E, S=T
97: M=T, N=C	98: Q=T, O=P	99: J=T, Z=G
100: B=T, H=E	101: R=A, Z=L	102: E=O, B=L
103: O=T, W=H	104: K=T, B=N	105: K=E, H=L
106: F=E, U=A	107: P=E, A=F	108: M=A, Y=H
109: Y=E, D=L	110: R=A, M=S	111: U=E, Y=V
112: M=A, C=N	113: U=H, B=R	114: G=E, M=T
115: X=I, P=M	116: C=T, R=U	117: L=O, K=W
118: K=A, J=B	119: F=N, G=S	120: R=N, D=O
121: U=T, B=H	122: P=I, D=A	123: M=O, V=T
124: W=I, F=M	125: E=T, V=I	126: X=A, P=Y
127: D=E, I=K	128: F=T, D=L	129: H=O, B=M
130: G=A, E=F	131: A=O, M=H	132: U=O, S=A

133: I=A, C=T	134: Z=E, W=M	135: G=A, I=S
136: T=N, P=S	137: O=T, S=M	138: D=E, I=G
139: M=T, F=C	140: C=E, G=R	141: A=O, U=F
142: L=R, H=N	143: T=A, Q=S	144: V=I, K=D
145: X=E, K=V	146: J=E, B=P	147: L=A, W=F
148: E=N, K=C	149: K=A, W=R	150: S=E, P=T
151: P=O, B=M	152: Q=E, K=C	153: E=N, T=R
154: O=I, E=T	155: C=T, S=K	156: R=E, P=S
157: W=I, Z=O	158: E=T, I=H	159: K=O, G=J
160: B=E, C=R	161: T=E, R=W	162: B=O, Z=C
163: D=R, H=F	164: N=O, W=M	165: Q=I, L=D
166: C=T, Z=G	167: H=O, P=T	168: H=A, X=D
169: P=T, L=W	170: L=T, K=N	171: R=T, S=J
172: N=E, Y=R	173: N=T, L=M	174: K=E, G=S
175: O=I, T=R	176: P=A, O=Y	177: E=T, A=N
178: L=E, W=H	179: I=E, J=O	180: Z=O, H=M
181: E=A, Z=K	182: S=T, H=K	183: B=N, A=D
184: D=A, L=C	185: P=N, T=E	186: U=R, B=A
187: Y=E, J=I	188: S=E, Y=M	189: I=O, N=R
190: K=O, L=M	191: O=S, E=A	192: F=O, P=I
193: L=T, A=C	194: W=R, C=E	195: G=N, V=M
196: C=E, D=L	197: O=E, B=N	198: H=T, P=O

199: R=T, N=A	200: M=O, N=D	201: B=A, M=C
202: Z=A, S=K	203: H=O, I=P	204: O=I, T=A
205: T=A, K=N	206: P=A, Y=E	207: M=O, N=E
208: S=A, Q=H	209: K=S, Q=A	210: B=E, R=L
211: F=E, J=U	212: S=I, Z=A	213: Y=A, G=C
214: M=A, H=S	215: R=S, U=T	216: X=A, S=I
217: R=E, Y=A	218: Q=S, E=C	219: K=I, V=G
220: V=E, R=G	221: B=O, T=R	222: L=R, K=O
223: H=W, G=R	224: S=N, L=T	225: H=O, G=P
226: D=O, A=S	227: G=I, L=T	228: E=O, U=H
229: D=E, Z=W	230: F=N, P=R	231: P=N, R=S
232: S=D, F=B	233: W=R, D=S	234: H=E, P=K
235: Z=D, N=T	236: M=I, B=H	237: Y=N, D=P
238: B=E, Z=I	239: U=I, E=A	240: X=A, J=I
241: X=A, O=Y	242: X=I, G=A	243: J=O, S=P
244: D=A, U=Y	245: N=H, J=E	246: Q=H, N=C
247: J=O, Q=E	248: X=E, H=N	249: Z=E, F=K
250: C=A, G=S	251: S=T, L=B	252: C=T, M=A
253: E=A, S=C	254: M=O, T=S	255: H=T, C=F
256: M=O, N=T	257: U=O, H=M	258: L=O, W=C
259: W=T, K=G	260: L=T, A=M	261: U=O, C=J
262: G=A, U=H	263: Q=R, J=E	264: J=I, O=S

265: K=I, H=E	266: S=T, P=M	267: T=I, V=L
268: D=E, B=O	269: I=E, L=A	270: V=I, F=O
271: X=R, U=I	272: W=I, E=K	273: L=T, Y=A
274: X=O, D=W	275: G=H, A=T	276: X=A, V=O
277: G=E, N=S	278: W=O, F=Y	279: F=I, H=O
280: D=I, W=A	281: V=N, T=B	282: C=A, F=L
283: O=D, N=B	284: Y=N, D=B	285: Y=E, A=O
286: W=E, Q=P	287: E=O, M=V	288: C=T, W=A
289: W=I, H=N	290: X=A, O=C	291: G=I, W=F
292: T=O, F=D	293: Y=N, E=K	294: F=O, H=I
295: P=A, C=I	296: Y=T, M=A	297: V=I, G=P
298: O=E, C=W	299: G=I, A=W	300: Q=N, X=T
301: K=T, M=D	302: J=O, L=W	303: G=E, S=O
304: N=E, B=R	305: G=E, N=I	306: Q=O, V=B
307: G=N, W=L	308: W=O, I=C	309: M=A, Q=H
310: G=O, R=P	311: U=S, K=H	312: Z=A, U=D
313: U=I, W=R	314: H=A, K=T	315: I=T, F=A
316: R=N, F=C	317: M=A, F=N	318: G=I, L=E
319: J=O, I=B	320: Y=E, T=L	321: V=O, N=C
322: L=I, G=V	323: K=I, Y=A	324: K=S, E=A
325: Z=N, J=T	326: S=T, M=R	327: S=I, D=A
328: D=T, C=O	329: J=E, S=D	330: L=T, J=E

331: L=I, C=A	332: X=H, K=S	333: K=A, W=O
334: F=E, D=T	335: O=N, J=L	336: X=I, B=D
337: D=T, G=K	338: V=A, R=M	339: B=T, D=L
340: Y=N, E=P	341: G=O, F=S	342: H=E, B=O
343: O=A, M=Y	344: D=E, X=O	345: A=D, M=S
346: C=E, J=M	347: W=H, Z=C	348: N=E, I=C
349: Y=O, M=E	350: G=S, H=E	351: L=E, U=D
352: G=S, J=D	353: S=R, H=A	354: T=N, Q=B
355: L=N, W=B	356: O=A, D=L	357: K=T, R=N
358: Y=A, W=T	359: S=R, A=F	360: R=O, F=C
361: D=N, U=E	362: W=M, B=E	363: I=E, A=F
364: M=N, P=A	365: E=N, H=S	366: L=T, K=F
367: G=O, I=S	368: X=E, A=K	369: F=N, U=L
370: T=E, X=D	371: I=R, D=A	372: F=I, Z=E
373: O=I, Z=S	374: C=E, A=I	375: X=N, P=K
376: G=O, U=T	377: Q=O, A=V	378: S=T, J=R
379: X=N, R=D	380: B=O, T=S	381: M=R, K=I
382: W=A, O=T	383: S=I, X=N	384: U=E, G=A
385: D=E, M=G	386: O=E, X=U	387: Y=O, I=A
388: L=I, Y=C	389: C=E, M=S	390: V=I, J=W
391: E=A, D=E	392: P=E, C=F	393: B=I, U=W
394: J=E, Y=F	395: P=I, V=N	396: R=I, N=V

397: G=I, D=L	398: M=E, R=T	399: M=O, F=E
400: C=E, L=W	401: E=T, V=B	402: Y=A, C=T
403: Q=O, R=I	404: B=E, O=I	405: B=E, H=A
406: Z=T, L=H	407: L=A, Q=Y	408: K=T, S=G
409: Z=A, T=E	410: V=O, Z=B	411: H=O, S=J
412: J=O, E=N	413: Z=I, R=C	414: B=S, K=A
415: M=I, A=B	416: D=T, S=M	417: B=T, Z=I
418: I=E, A=R	419: G=I, X=S	420: X=E, O=R
421: X=A, K=C	422: Q=E, H=A	423: M=O, W=I
424: W=T, Q=Y	425: C=E, K=L	426: N=O, T=D
427: R=S, N=E	428: X=A, P=I	429: R=I, N=G
430: U=O, A=T	431: D=E, K=W	432: R=T, Q=C
433: F=N, U=W	434: U=R, E=B	435: V=O, A=Y
436: N=S, V=A	437: D=A, G=H	438: S=E, X=C
439: U=A, D=R	440: M=O, L=B	441: L=A, T=E
442: G=A, V=T	443: C=O, T=W	444: U=T, C=N
445: R=O, V=N	446: X=E, Q=T	447: D=A, J=G
448: C=O, M=D	449: V=I, C=W	450: Z=A, I=Y
451: C=N, E=I	452: T=O, Q=M	453: G=E, D=H
454: Q=T, A=M	455: J=T, E=Q	456: K=E, H=T
457: A=E, O=W	458: O=I, H=D	459: U=E, L=J
460: A=T, L=C	461: Q=E, R=M	462: J=T, D=B

463: B=N, D=K	464: O=S, G=I	465: X=I, B=W
466: C=E, B=S	467: H=E, L=R	468: Y=T, Q=A
469: E=O, K=G	470: J=O, H=S	471: D=N, E=O
472: V=R, D=G	473: M=A, W=T	474: K=A, M=E
475: T=A, Z=S	476: C=N, R=A	477: G=O, B=I
478: F=T, W=H	479: B=E, A=M	480: L=A, P=S
481: U=A, O=L	482: W=A, O=E	483: H=E, W=L
484: X=N, Z=O	485: Q=E, G=P	486: V=T, B=I
487: J=N, A=I	488: I=E, Z=J	489: D=S, G=A
490: U=A, Q=S	491: A=N, J=R	492: Y=R, B=H
493: Q=E, P=O	494: L=N, A=R	495: A=I, M=L
496: B=A, Y=L	497: N=O, G=Y	498: C=O, N=S
499: R=A, G=W	500: J=N, O=U	

SOLUTIONS

1.

PAINTING IS EASY WHEN YOU DON'T KNOW HOW, BUT VERY DIFFICULT WHEN YOU DO. - EDGAR DEGAS

2.

IN DRAWING, ONE MUST LOOK FOR OR SUSPECT THAT THERE IS MORE THAN IS CASUALLY SEEN. - GEORGE BRIDGMAN

3.

YOU CAN'T CHEAT THE GAME. YOU CAN'T CHEAT THE GRIND. YOU GET OUT WHAT YOU PUT IN AT THE END OF THE DAY. - DABABY

4.

LOVE ISN'T SOMETHING YOU FIND. LOVE IS SOMETHING THAT FINDS YOU. - LORETTA YOUNG

5.

I CAN NEVER CONSENT TO BEING DICTATED TO. - JOHN TYLER

6.

AS YOU START TO WALK ON THE WAY, THE WAY APPEARS. - RUMI

7.

ART IS LONGING. YOU NEVER ARRIVE, BUT YOU KEEP GOING IN THE HOPE THAT YOU WILL. - ANSELM KIEFER

8.

A FRIEND IS SOMEONE WHO KNOWS ALL ABOUT YOU AND STILL LOVES YOU. - ELBERT HUBBARD

9.

NO ONE WOULD CHOOSE A FRIENDLESS EXISTENCE ON CONDITION OF HAVING ALL THE OTHER THINGS IN THE WORLD. - ARISTOTLE

10.

THE AMOUNT OF HAPPINESS THAT YOU HAVE DEPENDS ON THE AMOUNT OF FREEDOM YOU HAVE IN YOUR HEART. - THICH NHAT HANH

11.

DOUBT IS THE FATHER OF INVENTION. - GALILEO GALILEI

12.

IF IT'S A GOOD IDEA, GO AHEAD AND DO IT. IT'S EASIER TO ASK FORGIVENESS THAN IT IS TO GET PERMISSION. - GRACE HOPPER

13.

WE HAVE TO CONTINUALLY BE JUMPING OFF CLIFFS AND DEVELOPING OUR WINGS ON THE WAY DOWN. - KURT VONNEGUT

14.

POP CHANGES WEEK TO WEEK, MONTH TO MONTH. BUT GREAT MUSIC IS LIKE LITERATURE. - RAVI SHANKAR

15.

LITERATURE IS ONE OF THE MOST INTERESTING AND SIGNIFICANT EXPRESSIONS OF HUMANITY. - P. T. BARNUM

16.

ART WASHES AWAY FROM THE SOUL THE DUST OF EVERYDAY LIFE. - PABLO PICASSO

17.

TECHNOLOGICAL PROGRESS HAS MERELY PROVIDED US WITH MORE EFFICIENT MEANS FOR GOING BACKWARDS. - ALDOUS HUXLEY

18.

THE ACHILLES HEEL OF AN ARTIST LIES IN THE HOPE THAT HIS ART IS GOOD. - KAPIL GUPTA

19.

FRIENDSHIP NEEDS NO WORDS. IT IS SOLITUDE DELIVERED FROM THE ANGUISH OF LONELINESS. - DAG HAMMARSKJOLD

20.

THE READING OF ALL GOOD BOOKS IS LIKE A CONVERSATION WITH THE FINEST MINDS OF PAST CENTURIES. - RENE DESCARTES

21.

ANYTHING WORTH DYING FOR IS CERTAINLY WORTH LIVING FOR. - JOSEPH HELLER

22.

THERE ARE NO RULES FOR FRIENDSHIP. IT MUST BE LEFT TO ITSELF. WE CANNOT FORCE IT ANYMORE THAN LOVE. - WILLIAM HAZLITT

23.

AMERICAN HISTORY HAS FALLEN MORE AND MORE INTO THE HANDS OF ACADEMICS. - GORE VIDAL

24.

WE GO TO POETRY, WE GO TO LITERATURE IN GENERAL, TO BE FORWARDED WITHIN OURSELVES. - SEAMUS HEANEY

25.

THE ARTIST IS NOT A DIFFERENT KIND OF PERSON, BUT EVERY PERSON IS A DIFFERENT KIND OF ARTIST. - ERIC GILL

26.

IF YOUR ACTIONS INSPIRE OTHERS TO DREAM MORE, LEARN MORE, DO MORE AND BECOME MORE, YOU ARE A LEADER. - JOHN ADAMS

27.

SCIENCE IS THE GREAT ANTIDOTE TO THE POISON OF ENTHUSIASM AND SUPERSTITION. - ADAM SMITH

28.

IF THE TIMING'S RIGHT AND THE GODS ARE WITH YOU, SOMETHING SPECIAL HAPPENS. - RICK SPRINGFIELD

29.

YOU CAN'T GET MUCH DONE IN LIFE IF YOU ONLY WORK ON THE DAYS WHEN YOU FEEL GOOD. - JERRY WEST

30.

IF THERE'S A BOOK YOU REALLY WANT TO READ, BUT IT HASN'T BEEN WRITTEN YET, THEN YOU MUST WRITE IT. - TONI MORRISON

31.

GREAT LIVES NEVER GO OUT. THEY GO ON. - BENJAMIN HARRISON

32.

WHAT MAKES PHOTOGRAPHY A STRANGE INVENTION IS THAT ITS PRIMARY RAW MATERIALS ARE LIGHT AND TIME. - JOHN BERGER

33.

DON'T YOU KNOW THERE AIN'T NO DEVIL, IT'S JUST GOD WHEN HE'S DRUNK. - TOM WAITS

34.

HONESTY IS THE FIRST CHAPTER OF THE BOOK WISDOM. - THOMAS JEFFERSON

35.

A LITTLE FLATTERY WILL SUPPORT A MAN THROUGH GREAT FATIGUE. - JAMES MONROE

36.

IT'S SO FINE AND YET SO TERRIBLE TO STAND IN FRONT OF A BLANK CANVAS. - PAUL CEZANNE

37.

THE PAST IS A STEPPING STONE, NOT A MILLSTONE. - ROBERT PLANT

38.

THERE IS, OF COURSE, NO LARGER MASS HYSTERIA IN AMERICAN HISTORY THAN THE EPIDEMIC OF RACISM. - KEVIN YOUNG

39.

GREATNESS IS A LOT OF SMALL THINGS DONE WELL. - RAY LEWIS

40.

SOMETIMES YOU PUT WALLS UP NOT TO KEEP PEOPLE OUT, BUT TO SEE WHO CARES ENOUGH TO BREAK THEM DOWN. - SOCRATES

41.

WORKING HARD AND WORKING SMART SOMETIMES CAN BE TWO
DIFFERENT THINGS. - BYRON DORGAN

42.

NOW AND THEN IT'S GOOD TO PAUSE IN OUR PURSUIT OF HAPPINESS
AND JUST BE HAPPY. - GUILLAUME APOLLINAIRE

43.

I USED TO BE AN AMATEUR INVENTOR WHEN I WAS A KID. I'M ALWAYS
INVENTING SOMETHING. - ALAN ALDA

44.

IT'S NOT PAINFUL TO RELIVE IT. I'M COMFORTABLE WITH MY POSITION IN
AMERICAN HISTORY. - RODNEY KING

45.

ONE MAN PRACTICING SPORTSMANSHIP IS FAR BETTER THAN 50
PREACHING IT. - KNUTE ROCKNE

46.

YOU MAY THINK YOU KNOW WHO YOUR REAL FRIENDS ARE, BUT YOU
WON'T REALLY KNOW UNTIL YOU HIT ROCK BOTTOM. - UNKNOWN

47.

I JUST FIND MYSELF HAPPY WITH THE SIMPLE THINGS. APPRECIATING
THE BLESSINGS GOD GAVE ME. - DMX

48.

WHEN YOU'RE RIDING, ONLY THE RACE IN WHICH YOU'RE RIDING IS
IMPORTANT. - BILL SHOEMAKER

49.

EVERY RENAISSANCE COMES TO THE WORLD WITH A CRY, THE CRY OF THE HUMAN SPIRIT TO BE FREE. - ANNE SULLIVAN

50.

IF YOU THINK YOU HAVE IT TOUGH, READ HISTORY BOOKS. - BILL MAHER

51.

I HAVE COME TO BELIEVE THAT CARING FOR MYSELF IS NOT SELF-INDULGENT. IT IS AN ACT OF SURVIVAL. - AUDRE LORDE

52.

THE WORKS MUST BE CONCEIVED WITH FIRE IN THE SOUL BUT EXECUTED WITH CLINICAL COOLNESS. - JOAN MIRO

53.

I SAW THE ANGEL IN THE MARBLE AND CARVED UNTIL I SET HIM FREE. - MICHELANGELO

54.

NEVER THINK OF PAIN OR DANGER OR ENEMIES A MOMENT LONGER THAN IS NECESSARY TO FIGHT THEM. - AYN RAND

55.

IT'S EASIER TO DO A JOB RIGHT, THAN TO EXPLAIN WHY YOU DIDN'T. - MARTIN VAN BUREN

56.

WHEN ONCE THE ITCH OF LITERATURE COMES OVER A MAN, NOTHING CAN CURE IT BUT THE SCRATCHING OF A PEN. - SAMUEL LOVER

57.

I'M TRYING TO WRITE BOOKS THAT TASTE LIKE ICE CREAM BUT HAVE THE NUTRITION OF VEGETABLES. - DAN BROWN

58.

THE ARC OF THE MORAL UNIVERSE IS LONG, BUT IT BENDS TOWARD JUSTICE. – MARTIN LUTHER KING, JR.

59.

DON'T THINK ABOUT THE START OF THE RACE, THINK ABOUT THE ENDING. - USAIN BOLT

60.

THERE IS NO HAPPINESS EXCEPT IN THE REALIZATION THAT WE HAVE ACCOMPLISHED SOMETHING. - HENRY FORD

61.

OUR GREATEST GLORY IS NOT IN NEVER FALLING, BUT IN RISING EVERY TIME WE FALL. - CONFUCIUS

62.

EVERY ARTIST DIPS HIS BRUSH IN HIS OWN SOUL, AND PAINTS HIS OWN NATURE INTO HIS PICTURES. - HENRY WARD BEECHER

63.

I BELIEVE THAT A SCIENTIST LOOKING AT NONSCIENTIFIC PROBLEMS IS JUST AS DUMB AS THE NEXT GUY. - RICHARD P. FEYNMAN

64.

A BAD DAY DOESN'T CANCEL OUT A GOOD LIFE. KEEP GOING. - RICHIE NORTON

65.

EFFORTS AND COURAGE ARE NOT ENOUGH WITHOUT PURPOSE AND
DIRECTION. - JOHN F. KENNEDY

66.

DREAMS ARE ILLUSTRATIONS FROM THE BOOK YOUR SOUL IS WRITING
ABOUT YOU. - MARSHA NORMAN

67.

THERE WAS A TIME IN AMERICAN HISTORY WHEN ALMOST EVERY WHITE
PERSON KNEW WHO ARETHA FRANKLIN WAS. - PEABO BRYSON

68.

I'VE HAD THE SORT OF DAY THAT WOULD MAKE ST. FRANCIS OF ASSISI
KICK BABIES. - DOUGLAS ADAMS

69.

GREAT IS THE GUILT OF AN UNNECESSARY WAR. - JOHN ADAMS

70.

MONSTERS ARE REAL, GHOSTS ARE REAL, TOO. THEY LIVE INSIDE US,
AND SOMETIMES THEY WIN. - STEPHEN KING

71.

I HAVEN'T HAD A VERY GOOD DAY. I THINK I MIGHT STILL BE HUNGOVER
AND EVERYONE'S DEAD AND MY ROOT BEER'S GONE. - HOLLY B

72.

A TRUE ARTIST IS NOT ONE WHO IS INSPIRED, BUT ONE WHO INSPIRES
OTHERS. - SALVADOR DALI

73.

SOMETIMES IT'S THE JOURNEY THAT TEACHES YOU A LOT ABOUT YOUR DESTINATION. - DRAKE

74.

HAPPINESS DEPENDS MORE ON THE INWARD DISPOSITION OF MIND THAN ON OUTWARD CIRCUMSTANCES. - BENJAMIN FRANKLIN

75.

FIND THE PLACE INSIDE WHERE THERE IS JOY AND THE JOY WILL BURN OUT THE PAIN. - JOSEPH CAMPBELL

76.

EACH MOMENT IS A PLACE YOU'VE NEVER BEEN. - MARK STRAND

77.

YOU WERE BORN TO BE A PLAYER. YOU WERE MEANT TO BE HERE. THIS MOMENT IS YOURS. - HERB BROOKS

78.

MY IDEA OF HEAVEN IS TO WAKE UP, HAVE A GOOD BREAKFAST, AND SPEND THE REST OF THE DAY DRAWING. - PETER FALK

79.

SOMETIMES YOU JUST HAVE TO PUT ON LIP GLOSS AND PRETEND TO BE PSYCHED. - MINDY KALING

80.

SOME OF US THINK HOLDING ON MAKES US STRONG. BUT SOMETIMES IT IS LETTING GO. - HERMAN HESSE

81.

TALENT IS GOD GIVEN. BE HUMBLE. FAME IS MAN GIVEN. BE GRATEFUL. CONCEIT IS SELF GIVEN. BE CAREFUL. - JOHN WOODEN

82.

PAINTING FROM NATURE IS NOT COPYING THE OBJECT, IT'S REALISING ONE'S SENSATIONS. - PAUL CEZANNE

83.

THE PAINTER HAS THE UNIVERSE IN HIS MIND AND HANDS. - LEONARDO DA VINCI

84.

THERE IS NO SUBSTITUTE FOR BOOKS IN THE LIFE OF A CHILD. - MARY ELLEN CHASE

85.

YOU'RE NEVER A LOSER UNTIL YOU QUIT TRYING. - MIKE DITKA

86.

SHE READ BOOKS AS ONE WOULD BREATHE AIR, TO FILL UP AND LIVE. - ANNIE DILLARD

87.

YOU KNOW, HOBBES, SOME DAYS EVEN MY LUCKY ROCKETSHIP UNDERPANTS DON'T HELP. - BILL WATTERSON

88.

THE ADVANCEMENT AND DIFFUSION OF KNOWLEDGE IS THE ONLY GUARDIAN OF TRUE LIBERTY. - JAMES MADISON

89.

I AM A SLOW WALKER, BUT I NEVER WALK BACKWARDS. - ABRAHAM LINCOLN

90.

MY BAD HABITS AREN'T MY TITLE. MY STRENGTHS AND MY TALENT ARE MY TITLE. - LAYNE STALEY

91.

THE SECRET OF HAPPINESS IS TO COUNT YOUR BLESSINGS WHILE OTHERS ARE ADDING UP THEIR TROUBLES. - WILLIAM PENN

92.

IT IS NOT THE SIZE OF A MAN BUT THE SIZE OF HIS HEART THAT MATTERS. - EVANDER HOLYFIELD

93.

SOMETIMES, WHAT YOU'RE LOOKING FOR IS ALREADY THERE. - ARETHA FRANKLIN

94.

THE OBJECT OF LOVE IS TO SERVE, NOT TO WIN. - WOODROW WILSON

95.

IT'S NOT THE DESTINATION THAT MATTERS. IT'S THE CHANGE OF SCENE. - BRIAN ENO

96.

REMEMBER THAT HAPPINESS IS A WAY OF TRAVEL, NOT A DESTINATION. - ROY GOODMAN

97.

THE ART CHALLENGES THE TECHNOLOGY, AND THE TECHNOLOGY
INSPIRES THE ART. - JOHN LASSETER

98.

A PEOPLE WITHOUT THE KNOWLEDGE OF THEIR PAST HISTORY, ORIGIN
AND CULTURE IS LIKE A TREE WITHOUT ROOTS. - MARCUS GARVEY

99.

JUST KEEP GOING. EVERYBODY GETS BETTER IF THEY KEEP AT IT. - TED
WILLIAMS

100.

EVERYONE CHASES AFTER HAPPINESS, NOT NOTICING THAT HAPPINESS
IS RIGHT AT THEIR HEELS. - BERTOLT BRECHT

101.

BY LOOKING INTO MORE DETAILS OF AMERICAN HISTORY, WE CAN MAKE
MORE SENSE OF WHAT'S HAPPENING TODAY. - CHRISTOPH WALTZ

102.

A LEADERSHIP IS SOMEONE WHO BRINGS PEOPLE TOGETHER. - GEORGE
W. BUSH

103.

INDOLENCE IS A DELIGHTFUL BUT DISTRESSING STATE, WE MUST BE
DOING SOMETHING TO BE HAPPY. - MAHATMA GANDHI

104.

YOU MIGHT NOT BE ABLE TO OUTTHINK, OUT MARKET OR OUTSPEND
YOUR COMPETITION, BUT YOU CAN OUTWORK THEM. - LOU HOLTZ

105.

HE WHO SOWS COURTESY, REAPS FRIENDSHIP. HE WHO PLANTS KINDNESS, GATHERS LOVE. - SAINT BASIL

106.

BOOKS ARE THE BLESSED CHLOROFORM OF THE MIND. - OSWALD CHAMBERS

107.

THE WHOLE WESTWARD EXPANSION MYTH IS SEEN AS ROMANTIC. BUT IT'S A JOKE, A BLOT ON AMERICAN HISTORY. - FRANK WATERS

108.

THE MOST HUMAN THING ABOUT US IS OUR TECHNOLOGY. - MARSHALL MCLUHAN

109.

I BEGAN LEARNING THAT THOSE WHO ARE HAPPIEST ARE THOSE WHO DO THE MOST FOR OTHERS. - BOOKER T. WASHINGTON

110.

LIFE BEATS DOWN AND CRUSHES THE SOUL AND ART REMINDS YOU THAT YOU HAVE ONE. - STELLA ADLER

111.

HISTORY IS A PACK OF LIES WE PLAY ON THE DEAD. - VOLTAIRE

112.

PEOPLE ARE TRAPPED IN HISTORY AND HISTORY IS TRAPPED IN THEM. - JAMES BALDWIN

113.

THE REAL PROBLEM IS NOT WHETHER MACHINES THINK BUT WHETHER MEN DO. - B. F. SKINNER

114.

A LIE CAN RUN AROUND THE WORLD BEFORE THE TRUTH CAN GET ITS BOOTS ON. - JAMES WATT

115.

NOTHING CAN DIM THE LIGHT THAT SHINES FROM WITHIN. - MAYA ANGELOU

116.

INNOVATION IS THE OUTCOME OF A HABIT, NOT A RANDOM ACT. - SUKANT RATNAKAR

117.

I HAVE NOT FAILED. I HAVE JUST FOUND 10,000 WAYS THAT WON'T WORK. - THOMAS EDISON

118.

ANY FOOLISH BOY CAN STAMP ON A BEETLE, BUT ALL THE PROFESSORS IN THE WORLD CANNOT MAKE A BEETLE. - ARTHUR SCHOPENHAUER

119.

WHEN YOU'VE SEEN BEYOND YOURSELF, THEN YOU MAY FIND, PEACE OF MIND IS WAITING THERE. - GEORGE HARRISON

120.

IF TYRANNY AND OPPRESSION COME TO THIS LAND IT WILL BE IN THE GUISE OF FIGHTING A FOREIGN ENEMY. - JAMES MADISON

121.

CONFLICT WITH THE UNITED STATES IS ONE OF THE OVERWHELMING FACTS OF LATIN AMERICAN HISTORY. - STEPHEN KINZER

122.

ANYTHING THAT WON'T SELL, I DON'T WANT TO INVENT. ITS SALE IS PROOF OF UTILITY, AND UTILITY IS SUCCESS. - THOMAS EDISON

123.

HAPPINESS IS NOT SOMETHING YOU POSTPONE FOR THE FUTURE. IT IS SOMETHING YOU DESIGN FOR THE PRESENT. - JIM ROHN

124.

IN THE MIND OF EVERY ARTIST THERE IS A MASTERPIECE. - KAI GREENE

125.

IF EVERYTHING IS GOD'S WILL, THEN SO IS THE INVENTION OF THE VACCINE, JUST LIKE THE SEATBELT. - ELS BORST

126.

TECHNOLOGY IS ANYTHING THAT WASN'T AROUND WHEN YOU WERE BORN. - ALAN KAY

127.

SCIENCE IS MAGIC THAT WORKS. - KURT VONNEGUT

128.

IT TAKES A GREAT DEAL OF HISTORY TO PRODUCE A LITTLE LITERATURE. - HENRY JAMES

129.

IF YOU DO THE WORK YOU GET REWARDED. THERE ARE NO SHORTCUTS IN LIFE. - MICHAEL JORDAN

130.

THE FOUNDATION OF ALL TECHNOLOGY IS FIRE. - ISAAC ASIMOV

131.

WHERE A NEW INVENTION PROMISES TO BE USEFUL, IT OUGHT TO BE TRIED. - THOMAS JEFFERSON

132.

DON'T WASTE YOUR TIME ON JEALOUSY, SOMETIMES YOU'RE AHEAD, SOMETIMES YOU'RE BEHIND. - MARY SCHMICH

133.

TRUE LOVE IS LIKE GHOSTS, WHICH EVERYONE TALKS ABOUT AND FEW HAVE SEEN. - FRANCOIS DE LA ROCHEFOUCAULD

134.

THERE'S SO MUCH IN AMERICAN HISTORY THAT HAS BEEN HIDDEN AND SHUNNED. - ASHTON SANDERS

135.

A FALSE FRIEND AND A SHADOW ATTEND ONLY WHILE THE SUN SHINES. - BENJAMIN FRANKLIN

136.

SOONER OR LATER EVEN THE FASTEST RUNNERS HAVE TO STAND AND FIGHT. - STEPHEN KING

137.

TECHNOLOGY IS THE KNACK OF SO ARRANGING THE WORLD THAT WE DON'T HAVE TO EXPERIENCE IT. - MAX FRISCH

138.

THERE'S GOOD IN EVERYBODY. BOOST. DON'T KNOCK. - WARREN G. HARDING

139.

WE OVER ESTIMATE TECHNOLOGY IN THE SHORT TERM AND UNDER ESTIMATE TECHNOLOGY IN THE LONG TERM. - ARTHUR CLARKE

140.

LEARN THE RULES LIKE A PRO, SO YOU CAN BREAK THEM LIKE AN ARTIST. - PABLO PICASSO

141.

IF YOU FEEL GOOD ABOUT WHO YOU ARE INSIDE, IT WILL RADIATE. - PATTI SMITH

142.

HEROES MAY NOT BE BRAVER THAN ANYONE ELSE. THEY'RE JUST BRAVER FIVE MINUTES LONGER. - RONALD REAGAN

143.

WE ARE STUCK WITH TECHNOLOGY WHEN WHAT WE REALLY WANT IS JUST STUFF THAT WORKS. - DOUGLAS ADAMS

144.

I DON'T WANT TO NAME MY FANDOM; I WANT THEM TO NAME THEMSELVES. IF I'M COOL WITH IT, I'M COOL WITH IT. - DOJA CAT

145.

THE ARTIST SEES WHAT OTHERS ONLY CATCH A GLIMPSE OF. - LEONARDO DA VINCI

146.

BE PATIENT AND CALM. NO ONE CAN CATCH A FISH WITH ANGER. - HERBERT HOOVER

147.

A TRUE FRIEND IS ONE WHO WALKS ON A DIFFERENT PATH, BUT LIGHTS THE WAY WHEN DARKNESS CONCEALS YOUR DAY. - DODINSKY

148.

SCIENCE KNOWS NO COUNTRY, BECAUSE KNOWLEDGE BELONGS TO HUMANITY, AND IS THE TORCH WHICH ILLUMINATES THE WORLD. - LOUIS P

149.

PRACTICE WHAT YOU KNOW AND IT WILL HELP YOU TO MAKE CLEAR WHAT YOU DO NOT KNOW. - REMBRANDT

150.

A GREAT AGE OF LITERATURE IS PERHAPS ALWAYS A GREAT AGE OF TRANSLATIONS. - EZRA POUND

151.

ONE MACHINE CAN DO THE WORK OF FIFTY ORDINARY MEN. NO MACHINE CAN DO THE WORK OF ONE EXTRAORDINARY MAN. - ELBERT HUBBARD

152.

THE HIGHEST COMPLIMENT THAT YOU CAN PAY ME IS TO SAY THAT I WORK HARD EVERY DAY, THAT I NEVER DOG IT. - WAYNE GRETZKY

153.

INVENTION PRESUPPOSES IMAGINATION BUT SHOULD NOT BE CONFUSED WITH IT. - IGOR STRAVINSKY

154.

I BELIEVE IN THE DEVIL. I BELIEVE THERE'S A GOD, TOO. I MET GOD AT CHURCH - THE CATHOLIC CHURCH. - TRIPPIE REDD

155.

YOU ARE HAPPIEST WHILE YOU ARE MAKING THE GREATEST CONTRIBUTION. - ROBERT F. KENNEDY

156.

THE SAFE WAY TO DOUBLE YOUR MONEY IS TO FOLD IT OVER ONCE AND PUT IT IN YOUR POCKET. - KIN HUBBARD

157.

A ROOM WITHOUT BOOKS IS LIKE A BODY WITHOUT A SOUL. - MARCUS TULLIUS CICERO

158.

TRUST OUR HEART IF THE SEAS CATCH FIRE, LIVE BY LOVE THOUGH THE STARS WALK BACKWARDS. -E.E. CUMMINGS

159.

I DON'T THINK ABOUT TIME. YOU'RE HERE WHEN YOU'RE HERE. I THINK ABOUT TODAY, STAYING IN TUNE. - JOHN LEE HOOKER

160.

WORDS WITHOUT ACTIONS ARE THE ASSASSINS OF IDEALISM. - HERBERT HOOVER

161.

FRIENDSHIP IS A WORD, THE VERY SIGHT OF WHICH IN PRINT MAKES THE HEART WARM. - AUGUSTINE BIRRELL

162.

IF IT WEREN'T FOR PHILO T. FARNSWORTH, INVENTOR OF TV, WE'D STILL BE EATING FROZEN RADIO DINNERS. - JOHNNY CARSON

163.

TRULY GREAT FRIENDS ARE HARD TO FIND, DIFFICULT TO LEAVE, AND IMPOSSIBLE TO FORGET. - G. RANDOLPH

164.

NO MAN SHOULD ESCAPE OUR UNIVERSITIES WITHOUT KNOWING HOW LITTLE HE KNOWS. - J. ROBERT OPPENHEIMER

165.

NEVER WASTE A MINUTE THINKING ABOUT PEOPLE YOU DON'T LIKE. - DWIGHT D. EISENHOWER

166.

WE ARE ALL IN THE GUTTER, BUT SOME OF US ARE LOOKING AT THE STARS. - OSCAR WILDE

167.

SCHOOLS DON'T TEACH AMERICAN HISTORY THAT WELL, ESPECIALLY A LOT OF BLACK AMERICAN HISTORY. - COLSON WHITEHEAD

168.

FOR ME DRAWING IS AN ATTEMPT TO UNDERSTAND WHAT I FEEL ABOUT THE WORLD I LIVE IN. - BRIAN FROUD

169.

THE WORLD ALWAYS SEEMS BRIGHTER WHEN YOU'VE JUST MADE SOMETHING THAT WASN'T THERE BEFORE. - NEIL GAIMAN

170.

I NEVER PICK UP AN ITEM WITHOUT THINKING OF HOW I MIGHT IMPROVE IT. - THOMAS A. EDISON

171.

EVERY ACCOMPLISHMENT STARTS WITH THE DECISION TO TRY. - JOHN F. KENNEDY

172.

IF YOU ENJOY THE FRAGRANCE OF A ROSE, YOU MUST ACCEPT THE THORNS WHICH IT BEARS. - ISAAC HAYES

173.

HAPPINESS IS NOT A MATTER OF EVENTS, IT DEPENDS UPON THE TIDES OF THE MIND. - ALICE MEYNELL

174.

THE SCIENTIST IS NOT A PERSON WHO GIVES THE RIGHT ANSWERS, HE IS ONE WHO ASKS THE RIGHT QUESTIONS. - CLAUDE LEVI-STRAUSS

175.

NEVER QUESTION ANOTHER MAN'S MOTIVE. HIS WISDOM, YES, BUT NOT HIS MOTIVES. – DWIGHT D. EISENHOWER

176.

DRAWING MAKES YOU SEE THINGS CLEARER, AND CLEARER AND CLEARER STILL, UNTIL YOUR EYES ACHE. - DAVID HOCKNEY

177.

THERE IS NOTHING ON THIS EARTH MORE TO BE PRIZED THAN TRUE FRIENDSHIP. - THOMAS AQUINAS

178.

IT'S IN LITERATURE THAT TRUE LIFE CAN BE FOUND. IT'S UNDER THE MASK OF FICTION THAT YOU CAN TELL THE TRUTH. - GAO X

179.

PERHAPS ONE DID NOT WANT TO BE LOVED SO MUCH AS TO BE UNDERSTOOD. - GEORGE ORWELL

180.

THE ANSWERS YOU GET FROM LITERATURE DEPEND ON THE QUESTIONS YOU POSE. - MARGARET ATWOOD

181.

WHAT KEEPS MY HEART AWAKE IS COLOURFUL SILENCE. - CLAUDE MONET

182.

I'M NOT A FAN OF PUBLIC SCHOOL AT ALL. I THINK IT'S ONE OF THE GREATEST CATASTROPHES OF AMERICAN HISTORY. - KRS ONE

183.

YOU CAN'T KNOCK ON OPPORTUNITY'S DOOR AND NOT BE READY. - BRUNO MARS

184.

ALL CREATIVE PEOPLE WANT TO DO THE UNEXPECTED. - HEDY LAMARR

185.

IT IS ONLY WHEN WE ARE NO LONGER FEARFUL THAT WE BEGIN TO CREATE. - J. M. W. TURNER

186.

SCIENCE CAN NEVER SOLVE ONE PROBLEM WITHOUT RAISING TEN MORE PROBLEMS. – GEORGE BERNARD SHAW

187.

JUST AS HOUSES ARE MADE OF STONES, SO IS SCIENCE MADE OF FACTS. - HENRI POINCARE

188.

THE BEST INVENTIONS ARE USUALLY MADE BY OUTSIDERS UNAWARE OF WHAT "CAN'T BE DONE". - MARTIN MANN

189.

READING IS A CONVERSATION. ALL BOOKS TALK. BUT A GOOD BOOK LISTENS AS WELL. - MARK HADDON

190.

BLOOD ALONE MOVES THE WHEELS OF HISTORY. - MARTIN LUTHER

191.

EVERY PICTURE SHOWS A SPOT WITH WHICH THE ARTIST HAS FALLEN IN LOVE. - ALFRED SISLEY

192.

LET'S GO INVENT TOMORROW INSTEAD OF WORRYING ABOUT WHAT HAPPENED YESTERDAY. - STEVE JOBS

193.

IT'S AMAZING WHAT YOU CAN ACCOMPLISH IF YOU DO NOT CARE WHO GETS THE CREDIT. - HARRY S. TRUMAN

194.

HISTORY IS MERELY A LIST OF SURPRISES. IT CAN ONLY PREPARE US TO BE SURPRISED YET AGAIN. - KURT VONNEGUT

195.

THE DIFFERENCES BETWEEN FRIENDS CANNOT BUT REINFORCE THEIR FRIENDSHIP. – MAO TSE-TUNG

196.

CHAMPIONS KEEP PLAYING UNTIL THEY GET IT RIGHT. - BILLIE JEAN KING

197.

VICTORY IS IN HAVING DONE YOUR BEST. IF YOU'VE DONE YOUR BEST, YOU'VE WON. - BILLY BOWERMAN

198.

IT TAKES A GREAT DEAL OF COURAGE TO SEE THE WORLD IN ALL ITS TAINTED GLORY, AND STILL LOVE IT. - OSCAR WILDE

199.

WE WILL HAVE A TOTAL CHAOS WITHOUT BOOKS, LITERATURE, AND LIBRARY. - ANNE WALDMAN

200.

THE ONLY WAY NOT TO THINK ABOUT MONEY IS TO HAVE A GREAT DEAL OF IT. - EDITH WHARTON

201.

I CAN BE CHANGED BY WHAT HAPPENS TO ME. BUT I REFUSE TO BE REDUCED BY IT. - MAYA ANGELOU

202.

THE CYNICS MAY BE THE LOUDEST VOICES BUT I PROMISE YOU THEY WILL ACCOMPLISH THE LEAST. - BARACK OBAMA

203.

I DON'T PLAN ON BEING DISAPPOINTED. WE PLAN ON BEING REALLY GOOD, AND OBVIOUSLY, WE PLAN ON WINNING. - GREGG TROY

204.

PAINTING IS JUST ANOTHER WAY OF KEEPING A DIARY. - PABLO PICASSO

205.

LEAVE NOTHING FOR TOMORROW WHICH CAN BE DONE TODAY. - ABRAHAM LINCOLN

206.

MUSIC WASHES AWAY FROM THE SOUL THE DUST OF EVERYDAY LIFE. - BERTHOLD AUERBACH

207.

THERE IS NO 20 YEAR PERIOD IN AMERICAN HISTORY WHEN STOCKS LOST MONEY. - P. J. O'ROURKE

208.

IT HAS BECOME APPALLINGLY OBVIOUS THAT OUR TECHNOLOGY HAS EXCEEDED OUR HUMANITY. - ALBERT EINSTEIN

209.

THE KEY TO SUCCESS FOR EVERYTHING IN BUSINESS, SCIENCE AND TECHNOLOGY IS NEVER TO FOLLOW THE OTHERS. - MASARU IBUKA

210.

AMERICAN LITERATURE HAS ALWAYS BEEN IMMIGRANT. - SALMAN RUSHDIE

211.

DEMAGOGUERY IS NOT UNKNOWN IN AMERICAN HISTORY. - MICHAEL BENNET

212.

FRIENDS SHOW THEIR LOVE IN TIMES OF TROUBLE, NOT IN HAPPINESS. - EURIPIDES

213.

WHEN YOU GO OUT, GO OUT WITH A BANG, ANYTHING YOU DO. - PLAYBOI CARTI

214.

INVENTING IS A COMBINATION OF BRAINS AND MATERIALS. THE MORE BRAINS YOU USE, THE LESS MATERIAL YOU NEED. - CHARLES F.

215.

NEVER WORRY ABOUT BEING OBSESSIVE. I LIKE OBSESSIVE PEOPLE. OBSESSIVE PEOPLE MAKE GREAT ART. - SUSAN SONTAG

216.

PERSISTENCE CAN CHANGE FAILURE INTO EXTRAORDINARY ACHIEVEMENT. - MATT BIONDI

217.

THE AIM OF ART IS TO REPRESENT NOT THE OUTWARD APPEARANCE OF THINGS, BUT THEIR INWARD SIGNIFICANCE. - ARISTOTLE

218.

SCIENCE IS A COLLECTION OF SUCCESSFUL RECIPES. - PAUL VALERY

219.

I'M COVERING THE WORST PRESIDENT IN AMERICAN HISTORY. - HELEN THOMAS

220.

GOD WILL NEVER GIVE YOU ANYTHING YOU CAN'T HANDLE, SO DON'T STRESS. - KELLY CLARKSON

221.

I DON'T READ BOOKS BY PEOPLE WHO HAVE BETRAYED THE MOTHERLAND. - VLADIMIR PUTIN

222.

GREAT WORKS ARE PERFORMED NOT BY STRENGTH BUT BY PERSEVERANCE. - SAMUEL JOHNSON

223.

A REAL FRIEND IS ONE WHO WALKS IN WHEN THE REST OF THE WORLD WALKS OUT. - WALTER WINCHELL

224.

ALL OF SCIENCE IS NOTHING MORE THAN THE REFINEMENT OF EVERYDAY THINKING. - ALBERT EINSTEIN

225.

DO WHAT YOU WANT TO TRY DOING. TAKE WHATEVER YOU GET OUT OF
IT AND HAVE FUN. - J HOPE

226.

THE MAN WHO IS SWIMMING AGAINST THE STREAM KNOWS THE
STRENGTH OF IT. - WOODROW WILSON

227.

TECHNOLOGY LIKE ART IS A SOARING EXERCISE OF THE HUMAN
IMAGINATION. - DANIEL BELL

228.

DO WHAT YOU CAN, WITH WHAT YOU HAVE, WHERE YOU ARE. -
THEODORE ROOSEVELT

229.

TRUE WEALTH IS NOT OF THE POCKET, BUT OF THE HEART AND OF THE
MIND. - KEVIN GATES

230.

EITHER WRITE SOMETHING WORTH READING OR DO SOMETHING WORTH
WRITING. - BENJAMIN FRANKLIN

231.

SCIENCE IS A WONDERFUL THING IF ONE DOES NOT HAVE TO EARN
ONE'S LIVING AT IT. - ALBERT EINSTEIN

232.

SO YOU HAD A BAD DAY. KICK IT ASIDE AND BE GRATEFUL FOR ONE LESS
BAD DAY TO PASS THROUGH. - RICHELLE E. GOODRICH

233.

THE CLEAREST WAY INTO THE UNIVERSE IS THROUGH A FOREST WILDERNESS. - JOHN MUIR

234.

AND NOW THAT YOU DON'T HAVE TO BE PERFECT, YOU CAN BE GOOD. - JOHN STEINBECK

235.

STAY FIRMLY IN YOUR PATH AND DARE. BE WILD TWO HOURS A DAY. - PAUL GAUGUIN

236.

BARACK OBAMA IS THE MOST ANTIBUSINESS PRESIDENT IN A GENERATION, PERHAPS IN AMERICAN HISTORY. - DINESH D'SOUZA

237.

MANY PEOPLE DIE AT 25 AND AREN'T BURIED UNTIL THEY ARE 75. - BENJAMIN FRANKLIN

238.

IT'S LACK OF FAITH THAT MAKES PEOPLE AFRAID OF MEETING CHALLENGES, AND I BELIEVED IN MYSELF. - MUHAMMAD ALI

239.

WHILE DRAWING I DISCOVER WHAT I REALLY WANT TO SAY. - DARIO FO

240.

IT'S NOT WHAT YOU LOOK AT THAT MATTERS, IT'S WHAT YOU SEE. - HENRY DAVID THOREAU

241.

THE FREEDOM FLAG IS A POWERFUL, PHYSICAL REMINDER OF ONE OF THE DARKEST DAYS IN AMERICAN HISTORY. - ABIGAIL SPANBERGER

242.

BLACK HISTORY IS AMERICAN HISTORY. YOU CANNOT TELL ONE STORY WITHOUT TELLING THE OTHER. - WILLIAM BARR

243.

MANY PEOPLE WILL WALK IN AND OUT OF YOUR LIFE, BUT ONLY TRUE FRIENDS WILL LEAVE FOOTPRINTS IN YOUR HEART. - ELEANOR R

244.

WHEN I WAS YOUNGER, I WAS ALWAYS TAUGHT NOT TO MAKE EXCUSES. - DEREK JETER

245.

WHEREVER THEY BURN BOOKS THEY WILL ALSO, IN THE END, BURN HUMAN BEINGS. - HEINRICH HEINE

246.

NO MATTER THE CIRCUMSTANCES THAT YOU MAY BE GOING THROUGH, JUST PUSH THROUGH IT. - RAY LEWIS

247.

THE SCIENCE OF TODAY IS THE TECHNOLOGY OF TOMORROW. - EDWARD TELLER

248.

NO LOVE, NO FRIENDSHIP CAN CROSS THE PATH OF OUR DESTINY WITHOUT LEAVING SOME MARK ON IT FOREVER. - FRANCOIS MAURIAC

249.

WHEN SOMETHING IS IMPORTANT ENOUGH, YOU DO IT EVEN IF THE ODDS ARE NOT IN YOUR FAVOUR. - ELON MUSK

250.

THERE IS ALWAYS SOMETHING LEFT TO LOVE. - GABRIEL GARCA MRQUEZ

251.

IT'S BETTER TO FAIL AIMING HIGH THAN TO SUCCEED AIMING LOW. - BILL NICHOLSON

252.

IT IS IN LITERATURE THAT THE CONCRETE OUTLOOK OF HUMANITY RECEIVES ITS EXPRESSION. - ALFRED NORTH WHITEHEAD

253.

I AM A CONTRADICTORY MESS BUT I SEE IT AS MY PREROGATIVE TO CHANGE MY MOOD LIKE THE WEATHER. - SHIRLEY MANSON

254.

THE MAN WHO HAS NO SENSE OF HISTORY, IS LIKE A MAN WHO HAS NO EARS OR EYES. - ADOLF HITLER

255.

TRY AND FAIL, BUT DON'T FAIL TO TRY. - JOHN QUINCY ADAMS

256.

YOU HAVE TO EXPECT THINGS OF YOURSELF BEFORE YOU CAN DO THEM. - MICHAEL JORDAN

257.

OBSERVATION MORE THAN BOOKS AND EXPERIENCE MORE THAN PERSONS, ARE THE PRIME EDUCATORS. - AMOS BRONSON ALCOTT

258.

EDUCATION IS THE KEY TO UNLOCK THE GOLDEN DOOR OF FREEDOM. - GEORGE WASHINGTON CARVER

259.

TONY KAYE IS GREAT WITH THAT KIND OF STUFF. UP UNTIL AMERICAN HISTORY X, HE HAD ONLY DONE COMMERCIALS. - ETHAN SUPLEE

260.

YOU CAN'T PUT A LIMIT ON ANYTHING. THE MORE YOU DREAM, THE FARTHER YOU GET. - MICHAEL PHELPS

261.

MUSIC HAS HEALING POWER. IT HAS THE ABILITY TO TAKE PEOPLE OUT OF THEMSELVES FOR A FEW HOURS. - ELTON JOHN

262.

IF I CREATE FROM THE HEART, NEARLY EVERYTHING WORKS, IF FROM THE HEAD, ALMOST NOTHING. - MARC CHAGALL

263.

IT'S HARD TO BEAT A PERSON WHO NEVER GIVES UP. HEROES GET REMEMBERED, BUT LEGENDS NEVER DIE. - BABE RUTH

264.

MOST OF THE BEST MUSIC IN AMERICAN HISTORY WAS MADE BY PEOPLE WITH NO OPTIONS. - ISAAC BROCK

265.

WHEN I GET A LITTLE MONEY I BUY BOOKS, AND IF ANY IS LEFT I BUY FOOD AND CLOTHES. - DESIDERIUS ERASMUS

266.

ONE OF THE MOST BEAUTIFUL QUALITIES OF TRUE FRIENDSHIP IS TO UNDERSTAND AND TO BE UNDERSTOOD. - SENECA

267.

THERE IS A SINGLE LIGHT OF SCIENCE, AND TO BRIGHTEN IT ANYWHERE IS TO BRIGHTEN IT EVERYWHERE. - ISAAC ASIMOV

268.

JUST BECAUSE SOMETHING DOESN'T DO WHAT YOU PLANNED IT TO DO DOESN'T MEAN IT'S USELESS. - THOMAS EDISON

269.

ONE MUST ALWAYS DRAW, DRAW WITH THE EYES, WHEN ONE CANNOT DRAW WITH A PENCIL. - BALTHUS

270.

LOVE IS NOT ONLY SOMETHING YOU FEEL, IT IS SOMETHING YOU DO. - DAVID WILKERSON

271.

THERE ARE FEW INSTANCES WHEN AMERICAN HISTORY OFFERS US TWO CLEAR SIDES OF A MORAL LINE. - JOY REID

272.

WITHOUT KNOWLEDGE ACTION IS USELESS AND KNOWLEDGE WITHOUT ACTION IS FUTILE. - ABU BAKR

273.

THOSE WHO DO NOT WANT TO IMITATE ANYTHING PRODUCE NOTHING. - SALVADOR DALI

274.

LIFE IS NEVER FAIR, AND PERHAPS IT IS A GOOD THING FOR MOST OF US THAT IT IS NOT. - OSCAR WILDE

275.

IT IS ONLY WHEN THEY GO WRONG THAT MACHINES REMIND YOU HOW POWERFUL THEY ARE. - CLIVE JAMES

276.

I GREW UP IN THE SOUTH, SO A HUGE PART OF OUR AMERICAN HISTORY EDUCATION REVOLVED AROUND THE CIVIL WAR. - ANSON MOUNT

277.

LITERATURE COULD BE SAID TO BE A SORT OF DISCIPLINED TECHNIQUE FOR AROUSING CERTAIN EMOTIONS. - IRIS MURDOCH

278.

DO YOU KNOW WHAT MY FAVORITE PART OF THE GAME IS? THE OPPORTUNITY TO PLAY. - MIKE SINGLETARY

279.

THE KEY IS NOT THE WILL TO WIN. EVERYBODY HAS THAT. IT IS THE WILL TO PREPARE TO WIN THAT IS IMPORTANT. - BOBBY KNIGHT

280.

I'VE ALWAYS SPENT MORE TIME WITH A SMILE ON MY FACE THAN NOT, BUT THE THING IS, I DON'T WRITE ABOUT IT. - ROBERT SMITH

281.

NOBODY EVER WENT BROKE UNDERESTIMATING THE TASTE OF THE AMERICAN PUBLIC. - H. L MENCKEN

282.

I AM AN ANGLO-CATHOLIC IN RELIGION, A CLASSICIST IN LITERATURE AND A ROYALIST IN POLITICS. - T. S. ELIOT

283.

THE ONLY DIFFERENCE BETWEEN A GOOD DAY AND A BAD DAY IS YOUR ATTITUDE. - DENNIS S. BROWN

284.

A CHAMPION IS AFRAID OF LOSING. EVERYONE ELSE IS AFRAID OF WINNING. - BILLIE JEAN KING

285.

MOVIES ARE A COMPLICATED COLLISION OF LITERATURE, THEATRE, MUSIC AND ALL THE VISUAL ARTS. - YAHOO SERIOUS

286.

THE PRODUCTION OF TOO MANY USEFUL THINGS RESULTS IN TOO MANY USELESS PEOPLE. - KARL MARX

287.

I DO NOT FEAR COMPUTERS. I FEAR LACK OF THEM. - ISAAC ASIMOV

288.

ETHICAL TEACHING IS WEAKENED IF IT IS TIED UP WITH DOGMAS THAT WILL NOT BEAR EXAMINATION. - MARGARET E. KNIGHT

289.

SCIENCE ENRICHES THE MIND. LITERATURE ENRICHES THE
PERSONALITY. - NICOLAS GOMEZ DAVILA

290.

ADVERSITY CAUSES SOME MEN TO BREAK BUT OTHERS TO BREAK
RECORDS. - WILLIAM A. WARD

291.

WALKING WITH A FRIEND IN THE DARK IS BETTER THAN WALKING ALONE
IN THE LIGHT. - HELEN KELLER

292.

NEVER GIVE UP ON SOMEONE WHO IS HAVING A BAD DAY. TOMORROW
COULD BE YOURS. - GIOVANNIE DE SADELEER

293.

ONE PERSON CAN MAKE A DIFFERENCE, AND EVERYONE SHOULD TRY. -
JOHN F. KENNEDY

294.

TO INVENT, YOU NEED A GOOD IMAGINATION AND A PILE OF JUNK. -
THOMAS EDISON

295.

POLITICAL VITRIOL IS A FAMILIAR ENOUGH CHARACTERISTIC OF
AMERICAN HISTORY. - ROBERT DALLEK

296.

TOMORROW IS ALWAYS FRESH, WITH NO MISTAKES IN IT YET. - L. M.
MONTGOMERY

297.

THE GREATER OPPORTUNITY ENABLED ME TO MAKE IMPORTANT DISCOVERIES AND INVENTIONS. - PHILIP EMEAGWALI

298.

THE SHORT SUCCESSES THAT CAN BE GAINED IN A BRIEF TIME AND WITHOUT DIFFICULTY ARE NOT WORTH MUCH. - HENRY FORD

299.

I FEEL LIKE WHATEVER IS MEANT IS MEANT. I FEEL LIKE THIS IS ALREADY WRITTEN. - LIL BABY

300.

IRAQ IS GOING TO GO DOWN AS ONE OF THE GREATEST BLUNDERS IN AMERICAN HISTORY. - SCOTT ANDERSON

301.

LET YOURSELF BE GUTTED. LET IT OPEN YOU. START THERE. - CHERYL STRAYED

302.

ACCOMPLISHMENT WILL PROVE TO BE A JOURNEY, NOT A DESTINATION. - DWIGHT D. EISENHOWER

303.

THE CONSTRUCTION OF THE UNIVERSE IS CERTAINLY VERY MUCH EASIER TO EXPLAIN THAN IS THAT OF THE PLANT. - GEORG CHRISTOPH

304.

NO ONE REALLY HAS A BAD LIFE. NOT EVEN A BAD DAY. JUST BAD MOMENTS. - REGINA BRETT

305.

CREATIVITY IS INTELLIGENCE HAVING FUN. - ALBERT EINSTEIN

306.

I DON'T KNOW WHERE I'M GOING FROM HERE, BUT I PROMISE IT WON'T BE BORING. - DAVID BOWIE

307.

ANYONE WHO HAS NEVER MADE A MISTAKE HAS NEVER TRIED ANYTHING NEW. - ALBERT EINSTEIN

308.

OUR CIVILIZATION IS SHIFTING FROM SCIENCE AND TECHNOLOGY TO RHETORIC AND LITIGATION. - MASON COOLEY

309.

AMERICAN HISTORY IS NOT CLEAN. - BEN FOUNTAIN

310.

MEN ARE NOT PRISONERS OF FATE, BUT ONLY PRISONERS OF THEIR OWN MINDS. - FRANKLIN D. ROOSEVELT

311.

LONELINESS ADDS BEAUTY TO LIFE. IT PUTS A SPECIAL BURN ON SUNSETS AND MAKES NIGHT AIR SMELL BETTER. - HENRY ROLLINS

312.

OUTSIDE OF A DOG, A BOOK IS A MAN'S BEST FRIEND. INSIDE OF A DOG, IT'S TOO DARK TO READ. - GROUCHO MARX

313.

RELIGION IS NEVER THE PROBLEM. IT'S THE PEOPLE WHO USE IT TO GAIN POWER. - JULIAN CASABLANCAS

314.

IN LITERATURE AS IN LOVE, WE ARE ASTONISHED AT WHAT IS CHOSEN BY OTHERS. - ANDRE MAUROIS

315.

I ALWAYS FELT THAT MY GREATEST ASSET WAS NOT MY PHYSICAL ABILITY, IT WAS MY MENTAL ABILITY. - BRUCE JENNER

316.

IF YOU DON'T HAVE CONFIDENCE, YOU'LL ALWAYS FIND A WAY NOT TO WIN. - CARL LEWIS

317.

SOME PEOPLE WANT IT TO HAPPEN, SOME WISH IT WOULD HAPPEN, OTHERS MAKE IT HAPPEN. - MICHAEL JORDAN

318.

LOVE IS LIKE AN HOURGLASS, WITH THE HEART FILLING UP AS THE BRAIN EMPTIES. - JULES RENARD

319.

IT IS BETTER TO OFFER NO EXCUSE THAN A BAD ONE. - GEORGE WASHINGTON

320.

LAUGH LOUDLY, LAUGH OFTEN, AND MOST IMPORTANT, LAUGH AT YOURSELF. - CHELSEA HANDLER

321.

HE WHO IS NOT COURAGEOUS ENOUGH TO TAKE RISKS WILL
ACCOMPLISH NOTHING IN LIFE. - MUHAMMAD ALI

322.

PAINTINGS HAVE A LIFE OF THEIR OWN THAT DERIVES FROM THE
PAINTER'S SOUL. - VINCENT VAN GOGH

323.

I'VE ALWAYS BEEN INTERESTED IN THE DEPRESSION AS THIS VERY
DRAMATIC PIVOTAL PERIOD IN AMERICAN HISTORY. - RON HOWARD

324.

CREATIVITY IS ALLOWING YOURSELF TO MAKE MISTAKES. ART IS
KNOWING WHICH ONES TO KEEP. - SCOTT ADAMS

325.

I DON'T WANT TO BE THE NEXT MICHAEL JORDAN, I ONLY WANT TO BE
KOBE BRYANT. - KOBE BRYANT

326.

EVERY DAY OF MY LIFE, I'M TRYING TO FIND A WAY TO GET BETTER. - RAY
LEWIS

327.

I DON'T BELIEVE IN ACCIDENTS. THERE ARE ONLY ENCOUNTERS IN
HISTORY. - PABLO PICASSO

328.

THE ONLY THING WE HAVE TO FEAR IS FEAR ITSELF. - FRANKLIN D.
ROOSEVELT

329.

IF I READ A BOOK AND IT MAKES MY WHOLE BODY SO COLD NO FIRE CAN EVER WARM ME, I KNOW THAT IS POETRY. - EMILY DICKINSON

330.

WHERE THE SPIRIT DOES NOT WORK WITH THE HAND, THERE IS NO ART. - LEONARDO DA VINCI

331.

THE GREAT MYTH OF OUR TIMES IS THAT TECHNOLOGY IS COMMUNICATION. - LIBBY LARSEN

332.

HAVE FAITH, HAVE FAITH. WHEN YOU HAVE NOTHING ELSE HAVE FAITH. - FRANCINE RIVERS

333.

THE GREAT OCEAN OF TRUTH LAY ALL UNDISCOVERED BEFORE ME. - ISAAC NEWTON

334.

CREATIVITY IS TAKING THE BEST SKILLS AND TECHNIQUES FROM EXPERTS AROUND YOU AND IMPROVING UPON THEM. - UNKNOWN

335.

IF I'M GONNA TELL A REAL STORY, I'M GONNA START WITH MY NAME. - KENDRICK LAMAR

336.

IN THE TIME OF DARKEST DEFEAT, VICTORY MAY BE NEAREST. - WILLIAM MCKINLEY

337.

IF IT KEEPS UP, MAN WILL ATROPHY ALL HIS LIMBS BUT THE PUSH-
BUTTON FINGER. - FRANK LLOYD WRIGHT

338.

DRAWING THINGS MAKES THEM SEEM MORE REAL AND MAKES ME FEEL
MORE ALIVE. - DAVID GENTLEMAN

339.

GREAT LITERATURE IS SIMPLY LANGUAGE CHARGED WITH MEANING TO
THE UTMOST POSSIBLE DEGREE. - EZRA POUND

340.

DO NOT PRAY FOR EASY LIVES, PRAY TO BE STRONGER MEN. - JOHN F.
KENNEDY

341.

I'M ONE OF THE MOST HUMBLE PEOPLE YOU'LL PROBABLY EVER MEET. -
SKI MASK THE SLUMP GOD

342.

ART IS NOT A HANDICRAFT; IT IS THE TRANSMISSION OF FEELING THE
ARTIST HAS EXPERIENCED. - LEO TOLSTOY

343.

IF YOU DO WHAT YOU LOVE, YOU'LL NEVER WORK A DAY IN YOUR LIFE. -
MARC ANTHONY

344.

ONCE A NEW TECHNOLOGY ROLLS OVER YOU, IF YOU'RE NOT PART OF
THE STEAMROLLER, YOU'RE PART OF THE ROAD. - STEWART BRAND

345.

TO BE GOOD, AND TO DO GOOD, IS ALL WE HAVE TO DO. - JOHN ADAMS

346.

ONE MAN WITH COURAGE MAKES A MAJORITY. - ANDREW JACKSON

347.

AN ATHLETE CANNOT RUN WITH MONEY IN HIS POCKETS. HE MUST RUN WITH HOPE IN HIS HEART AND DREAMS IN HIS HEAD. - EMIL Z

348.

LOYALTY TO THE COUNTRY ALWAYS. LOYALTY TO THE GOVERNMENT WHEN IT DESERVES IT. - MARK TWAIN

349.

THE ROLE OF THE TEACHER IS TO CREATE THE CONDITIONS FOR INVENTION RATHER THAN PROVIDE READY-MADE KNOWLEDGE. - SEYMOUR P

350.

I USED TO BE DISGUSTED. NOW I TRY TO BE AMUSED. - ELVIS COSTELLO

351.

AVIATION IS THE BRANCH OF ENGINEERING THAT IS LEAST FORGIVING OF MISTAKES. - FREEMAN DYSON

352.

THE ESSENCE OF TRUE FRIENDSHIP IS TO MAKE ALLOWANCE FOR ANOTHER'S LITTLE LAPSES. - DAVID STOREY

353.

ROCK AND ROLL HAS PROBABLY GIVEN MORE THAN IT'S TAKEN. - CHARLIE WATTS

354.

THE THINGS I WANT TO KNOW ARE IN BOOKS. MY BEST FRIEND IS THE MAN WHO'LL GET ME A BOOK I AIN'T READ. - ABRAHAM LINCOLN

355.

THERE ARE THREE FAITHFUL FRIENDS, AN OLD WIFE, AN OLD DOG, AND READY MONEY. - BENJAMIN FRANKLIN

356.

DRAWING IS LIKE MAKING AN EXPRESSIVE GESTURE, WITH THE ADVANTAGE OF PERMANENCE. - HENRI MATISSE

357.

WHAT NEW TECHNOLOGY DOES IS CREATE NEW OPPORTUNITIES TO DO A JOB THAT CUSTOMERS WANT DONE. - TIM O'REILLY

358.

I CANNOT EMPHASIZE THE IMPORTANCE OF A GOOD TEACHER. - TEMPLE GRANDIN

359.

A TRUE FRIEND IS SOMEONE WHO IS THERE FOR YOU WHEN HE'D RATHER BE ANYWHERE ELSE. - LEN WEIN

360.

TO AVOID CRITICISM SAY NOTHING, DO NOTHING, BE NOTHING. - ARISTOTLE

361.

INVENTION IS THE TALENT OF YOUTH, AS JUDGMENT IS OF AGE. - JONATHAN SWIFT

362.

I DESTROY MY ENEMIES WHEN I MAKE THEM MY FRIENDS. - ABRAHAM LINCOLN

363.

AN HONORABLE DEFEAT IS BETTER THAN A DISHONORABLE VICTORY. - MILLARD FILLMORE

364.

NO AMOUNT OF SKILLFUL INVENTION CAN REPLACE THE ESSENTIAL ELEMENT OF IMAGINATION. - EDWARD HOPPER

365.

LIFE IS TOUGH MY DARLING, BUT SO ARE YOU. - STEPHANIE BENNETT HENRY

366.

TRUE FRIENDSHIP COMES WHEN THE SILENCE BETWEEN TWO PEOPLE IS COMFORTABLE. - DAVID TYSON GENTRY

367.

ROCK SOLID BECAME THE SOLID FOUNDATION ON WHICH I REBUILT MY LIFE. - J.K. ROWLING

368.

THE KEY INGREDIENT TO ANY KIND OF HAPPINESS OR SUCCESS IS TO NEVER GIVE LESS THAN YOUR BEST. - RUSSELL SIMMONS

369.

NEVER LET YOUR HEAD HANG DOWN. NEVER GIVE UP AND SIT DOWN AND GRIEVE. FIND ANOTHER WAY. - SATCHEL PAIGE

370.

THE DECLARATION OF INDEPENDENCE IS A SACRED PART OF AMERICAN HISTORY. - PAUL GILLMOR

371.

MOST PEOPLE WOULD RATHER BE CERTAIN THEY'RE MISERABLE, THAN RISK BEING HAPPY. - ROBERT ANTHONY

372.

ONLY HE WHO CAN SEE THE INVISIBLE CAN DO THE IMPOSSIBLE. - FRANK L. GAINES

373.

HERBERT HOOVER VERSUS AL SMITH IN 1928 WAS ONE OF THE DIRTIEST ELECTIONS IN AMERICAN HISTORY. - JOSEPH CUMMINS

374.

THIS DAY HAD OFFICIALLY PUNCHED EVERY HOLE IN HER CRAZY TICKET. - KIMBERLY KINCAID

375.

YOU DON'T KNOW WHAT YOU CAN MISS BEFORE YOU TRY. - FRANKLIN PIERCE

376.

STRAIGHT ROADS DO NOT MAKE SKILLFUL DRIVERS. - PAULA COELHO

377.

LITERATURE IS STREWN WITH THE WRECKAGE OF MEN WHO HAVE MINDED BEYOND REASON THE OPINIONS OF OTHERS. - VIRGINIA WOOLF

378.

HE KNEW EVERYTHING ABOUT LITERATURE EXCEPT HOW TO ENJOY IT. - JOSEPH HELLER

379.

AN INVENTION HAS TO MAKE SENSE IN THE WORLD IT FINISHES IN, NOT IN THE WORLD IT STARTED. - TIM O'REILLY

380.

AN INVENTOR IS SIMPLY A FELLOW WHO DOESN'T TAKE HIS EDUCATION TOO SERIOUSLY. - CHARLES KETTERING

381.

LITERATURE LED ME TO FREEDOM, NOT THE OTHER WAY ROUND. - ISMAIL KADARE

382.

A THEATRE, A LITERATURE, AN ARTISTIC EXPRESSION THAT DOES NOT SPEAK FOR ITS OWN TIME HAS NO RELEVANCE. - DARIO FO

383.

I THINK THE AUTOMATION OF VISION IS A MUCH BIGGER DEAL THAN THE INVENTION OF PERSPECTIVE. - TREVOR PAGLEN

384.

YOU CAN BE THE MOON AND STILL BE JEALOUS OF THE STARS. - GARY ALLAN

385.

HAPPINESS GROWS AT OUR OWN FIRESIDES, AND IS NOT TO BE PICKED IN STRANGER'S GARDENS. - DOUGLAS JERROLD

386.

YOU'RE THE ONE WHO IS WEAK. YOU WILL NEVER KNOW LOVE OR FRIENDSHIP. AND I FEEL SORRY FOR YOU. - J. K. ROWLING

387.

THERE IS ONLY ONE PERSON WHO COULD EVER MAKE YOU HAPPY, AND THAT PERSON IS YOU. - DAVID BURNS

388.

THE CIRCULATION OF CONFIDENCE IS BETTER THAN THE CIRCULATION OF MONEY. - JAMES MADISON

389.

SCIENCE MAY SET LIMITS TO KNOWLEDGE, BUT SHOULD NOT SET LIMITS TO IMAGINATION. - BERTRAND RUSSELL

390.

NEWTON, OF COURSE, WAS THE INVENTOR OF DIFFERENTIAL CALCULUS SO HIS PLACE IN THE TALE IS QUITE SPECIAL. - KIT WILLIAMS

391.

THE SMALL PART OF IGNORANCE THAT WE ARRANGE AND CLASSIFY WE GIVE THE NAME OF KNOWLEDGE. - AMBROSE BIERCE

392.

VALUE FRIENDSHIP FOR WHAT THERE IS IN IT, NOT FOR WHAT CAN BE GOTTEN OUT OF IT. - H. CLAY TRUMBULL

393.

I DON'T WANT A BLACK HISTORY MONTH. BLACK HISTORY IS AMERICAN HISTORY. - MORGAN FREEMAN

394.

ONCE YOU FIGURE OUT WHAT RESPECT TASTES LIKE, IT TASTES BETTER THAN ATTENTION. BUT YOU HAVE TO GET THERE. - PINK

395.

CHALLENGES MAKE LIFE INTERESTING, HOWEVER OVERCOMING THEM IS WHAT MAKES LIFE MEANINGFUL. - MARK TWAIN

396.

THE ONLY PLACE SUCCESS COMES BEFORE WORK IS IN THE DICTIONARY. - VINCE LOMBARDI

397.

DON'T THREATEN ME WITH LOVE, BABY. LET'S JUST GO WALKING IN THE RAIN. - BILLIE HOLIDAY

398.

THERE'S JUST SOME MAGIC IN TRUTH AND HONESTY AND OPENNESS. - FRANK OCEAN

399.

WHEN YOU SEE A GOOD MOVE, LOOK FOR A BETTER ONE. - EMANUEL LASKER

400.

SCIENCE AND TECHNOLOGY ARE WHAT WE CAN DO. MORALITY IS WHAT WE AGREE WE SHOULD OR SHOULD NOT DO. - E. O. WILSON

401.

THE BOOKS THAT THE WORLD CALLS IMMORAL ARE BOOKS THAT SHOW THE WORLD ITS OWN SHAME. - OSCAR WILDE

402.

GOOD FRIENDS ARE LIKE STARS. YOU DON'T ALWAYS SEE THEM, BUT YOU KNOW THEY ARE ALWAYS THERE. - CONFUCIUS

403.

THE VOTING RIGHTS ACT OF 1965 BROUGHT AN END TO THE UGLY JIM CROW PERIOD IN AMERICAN HISTORY. - LISA MURKOWSKI

404.

WORRY IS THE INTEREST PAID BY THOSE WHO BORROW TROUBLE. - GEORGE WASHINGTON

405.

WHATEVER YOU ARE, BE A GOOD ONE. - ABRAHAM LINCOLN

406.

TO BE HAPPY, WE MUST NOT BE TOO CONCERNED WITH OTHERS. - ALBERT CAMUS

407.

I READ SO MANY BOOKS WHEN I WAS A KID THAT I DIDN'T EVEN KNOW WERE SHAPING ME UP. - STORMZY

408.

SET YOUR GOALS HIGH, AND DON'T STOP TILL YOU GET THERE. - BO JACKSON

409.

I'M REALLY LOOKING FORWARD TO SEEING WHAT LIFE BRINGS TO ME. - RIHANNA

410.

BARACK OBAMA IS ONE OF THE GREATEST POLITICIANS IN AMERICAN HISTORY. - JOHN PODHORETZ

411.

CONFORMITY IS THE JAILER OF FREEDOM AND THE ENEMY OF GROWTH. - JOHN F. KENNEDY

412.

YOU'LL NEVER FIND PEACE OF MIND UNTIL YOU LISTEN TO YOUR HEART. - GEORGE MICHAEL

413.

YOU CAN'T GIVE UP IN LIFE. YOU JUST CAN'T DO IT, NO MATTER WHAT IT IS THAT IS GOING ON. - JOEY JORDISON

414.

A SINGLE CONVERSATION ACROSS THE TABLE WITH A WISE MAN IS BETTER THAN TEN YEARS MERE STUDY OF BOOKS. - HENRY LONGFELLOW

415.

THE BEAUTIFUL THING ABOUT LEARNING IS NOBODY CAN TAKE IT AWAY FROM YOU. - B. B. KING

416.

AN ARTIST MUST HAVE HIS MEASURING TOOLS NOT IN THE HAND, BUT IN THE EYE. - MICHELANGELO

417.

DRAWING AT ITS BEST IS NOT WHAT YOUR EYES SEE BUT WHAT OUR MIND UNDERSTANDS. - MILLARD SHEETS

418.

YOU'VE GOT THE SUN, YOU'VE GOT THE MOON, AND YOU'VE GOT THE ROLLING STONES. - KEITH RICHARDS

419.

IT IS STRANGE HOW ONE FEELS DRAWN FORWARD WITHOUT KNOWING AT FIRST WHERE ONE IS GOING. - GUSTAV MAHLER

420.

ONE RULE OF INVENTION. BEFORE YOU CAN INVENT IT, YOU HAVE TO IMAGINE IT. - JAMES GUNN

421.

MY ATTITUDES HAVE CHANGED, BUT SOMEBODY WOULD HAVE TO READ ALL MY BOOKS TO FIND OUT HOW THEY HAVE. - IRWIN SHAW

422.

MOST FOLKS ARE ABOUT AS HAPPY AS THEY MAKE UP THEIR MINDS TO BE. - ABRAHAM LINCOLN

423.

DO NOT FEAR MISTAKES. YOU WILL KNOW FAILURE. CONTINUE TO REACH OUT. - BENJAMIN FRANKLIN

424.

YOU DON'T HAVE TO BURN BOOKS TO DESTROY A CULTURE. JUST GET PEOPLE TO STOP READING THEM. - RAY BRADBURY

425.

I DECIDED LONG AGO NEVER TO WALK IN ANYONE'S SHADOW. IF I FAIL, OR IF I SUCCEED AT LEAST I DID AS I BELIEVE. - WHITNEY H

426.

IF THERE'S ONE THING I'M GOOD AT, IT'S GATHERING PEOPLE TOGETHER TO DO SOMETHING FUN. - DAVE GROHL

427.

OF ALL THE THINGS I'VE LOST, I MISS MY MIND THE MOST. - OZZY OSBOURNE

428.

THERE IS NO GOOD DAY OR BAD DAY, ONLY GOOD OR BAD ACTIONS. - AMIT KALANTRI

429.

SCIENCE GIVES US KNOWLEDGE, BUT ONLY PHILOSOPHY CAN GIVE US WISDOM. - WILL DURANT

430.

IT'S NOT THAT WE USE TECHNOLOGY, WE LIVE TECHNOLOGY. - GODFREY REGGIO

431.

THE WORLD SPINS. WE STUMBLE ON. IT IS ENOUGH. - COLUM MCCANN

432.

THERE ARE CHORDS IN THE HEARTS OF THE MOST RECKLESS WHICH CANNOT BE TOUCHED WITHOUT EMOTION. - EDGAR ALLEN POE

433.

EVERYTHING IS HARD BEFORE IT IS EASY. - JOHANN WOLFGANG VON GOETHE

434.

BAD LITERATURE IS A FORM OF TREASON. - JOSEPH BRODSKY

435.

I'M A HISTORY BUFF, SO I'VE BEEN READING LOTS OF BOOKS ON IRISH AND AMERICAN HISTORY. - SHEAMUS

436.

THE SADDEST ASPECT OF LIFE NOW IS THAT SCIENCE GATHERS KNOWLEDGE FASTER THAN SOCIETY GATHERS WISDOM. - ISAAC ASIMOV

437.

IT'S ABOUT HAVING PERSONALITY. IT'S NOT ABOUT BEING THE BAD GUY, IT'S ABOUT ENTERTAINING PEOPLE. - FLOYD MAYWEATHER

438.

LITERATURE IS THE ART OF WRITING SOMETHING THAT WILL BE READ TWICE. JOURNALISM WHAT WILL BE GRASPED AT ONCE. - CYRIL C

439.

LIVE SIMPLY, LOVE GENEROUSLY, CARE DEEPLY, SPEAK KINDLY, LEAVE THE REST TO GOD. - RONALD REAGAN

440.

WHEN OUR MEMORIES OUTWEIGH OUR DREAMS, IT IS THEN THAT WE BECOME OLD. – BILL CLINTON

441.

HE COULDN'T BELIEVE IT WAS ONLY WEDNESDAY. AND IT WAS MADE WORSE WHEN HE REALIZED IT WAS ACTUALLY TUESDAY. - TJ KLUNE

442.

FINDING GOOD PLAYERS IS EASY. GETTING THEM TO PLAY AS A TEAM IS ANOTHER STORY. - CASEY STENGEL

443.

THE ONLY WAY TO HAVE A FRIEND IS TO BE ONE. - RALPH WALDO EMERSON

444.

NEVER PUT OFF UNTIL TOMORROW WHAT YOU CAN DO TODAY. - THOMAS JEFFERSON

445.

NATURE AND BOOKS BELONG TO THE EYES THAT SEE THEM. - RALPH WALDO EMERSON

446.

ON MATTERS OF STYLE, SWIM WITH THE CURRENT, ON MATTERS OF PRINCIPLE, STAND LIKE A ROCK. - THOMAS JEFFERSON

447.

I HAVE ALREADY SETTLED IT FOR MYSELF SO FLATTERY AND CRITICISM GO DOWN THE SAME DRAIN AND I AM QUITE FREE. - GEORGIA O

448.

TAKE CARE OF ALL YOUR MEMORIES. FOR YOU CANNOT RELIVE THEM. - BOB DYLAN

449.

A WORK OF ART WHICH DID NOT BEGIN IN EMOTION IS NOT ART. - PAUL CEZANNE

450.

A PERSON WHO CARES ABOUT THE EARTH WILL RESONATE WITH ITS PURITY. - SALLY FOX

451.

I'M NOT AN INVENTOR. I JUST WANT TO MAKE THINGS BETTER. - DANIEL EK

452.

NEVER CONFUSE THE SIZE OF YOUR PAYCHECK WITH THE SIZE OF YOUR TALENT. - MARLON BRANDO

453.

SCIENCE AND LITERATURE ARE NOT TWO THINGS, BUT TWO SIDES OF ONE THING. - THOMAS HUXLEY

454.

THE ARTIST MUST TRAIN NOT ONLY HIS EYE BUT ALSO HIS SOUL. - WASSILY KANDINSKY

455.

LITERATURE IS THE QUESTION MINUS THE ANSWER. - ROLAND BARTHES

456.

A TROPHY CARRIES DUST. MEMORIES LAST FOREVER. - MARY LOU RETTON

457.

IF YOU'RE WALKING DOWN THE RIGHT PATH AND YOU'RE WILLING TO KEEP WALKING, EVENTUALLY YOU'LL MAKE PROGRESS. - BARACK OBAMA

458.

THE DIFFERENCE BETWEEN GENIUS AND STUPIDITY IS, GENIUS HAS ITS LIMITS. – ALBERT EINSTEIN

459.

ARTISTS ARE JUST CHILDREN WHO REFUSE TO PUT DOWN THEIR CRAYONS. - AL HIRSCHFELD

460.

OUR ABILITY TO CREATE HAS OUTREACHED OUR ABILITY TO USE WISELY THE PRODUCTS OF OUR INVENTION. - WHITNEY M. YOUNG

461.

AFTER MAKING A MISTAKE OR SUFFERING A MISFORTUNE, THE MAN OF GENIUS ALWAYS GETS BACK ON HIS FEET. - NAPOLEON BONAPARTE

462.

TECHNOLOGY IS BEST WHEN IT BRINGS PEOPLE TOGETHER. - MATT MULLENWEG

463.

INVENTING IS A SKILL THAT SOME PEOPLE HAVE AND SOME PEOPLE DON'T. BUT YOU CAN LEARN HOW TO INVENT. - RAY DOLBY

464.

SCIENCE FINDS CURES MORE EASILY THAN ANSWERS. - JEAN ROSTAND

465.

I WANT TO GO DOWN IN THE HISTORY BOOKS WITH WHAT I'VE ACHIEVED.
- LANDO NORRIS

466.

LET US DARE TO READ, THINK, SPEAK AND WRITE. - JOHN ADAMS

467.

THE REWARD FOR WORK WELL DONE IS THE OPPORTUNITY TO DO MORE.
- JONAS SALK

468.

THE HARDER THE CONFLICT, THE GREATER THE TRIUMPH. - GEORGE
WASHINGTON

469.

NO MAN IS GOOD ENOUGH TO GOVERN ANOTHER MAN WITHOUT HIS
CONSENT. - ABRAHAM LINCOLN

470.

DON'T LET YOUR HAPPINESS DEPEND ON SOMETHING YOU MAY LOSE. -
C.S. LEWIS

471.

THE DECLINE OF LITERATURE INDICATES THE DECLINE OF A NATION. -
JOHANN WOLFGANG VON GOETHE

472.

TELL THE TRUTH, WORK HARD AND COME TO DINNER ON TIME. - GERALD
FORD

473.

RATHER THAN HUMANIZING TECHNOLOGY, MODERN MAN PREFERS TO TECHNIFY MAN. - NICOLAS GOMEZ DAVILA

474.

DRAWING IS NOT WHAT ONE SEES, BUT WHAT ONE CAN MAKE OTHERS SEE. - EDGAR DEGAS

475.

ANY SUFFICIENTLY ADVANCED TECHNOLOGY IS INDISTINGUISHABLE FROM MAGIC. - ARTHUR CLARKE

476.

NEARLY ALL MEN CAN STAND ADVERSITY, BUT IF YOU WANT TO TEST A MAN'S CHARACTER, GIVE HIM POWER. - ABRAHAM LINCOLN

477.

IF PEOPLE ONLY KNEW HOW HARD I WORK TO GAIN MY MASTERY. IT WOULDN'T SEEM SO WONDERFUL AT ALL. – MICHELANGELO

478.

IT IS HARD TO FAIL, BUT IT IS WORSE NEVER TO HAVE TRIED TO SUCCEED. - THEODORE ROOSEVELT

479.

NEVER DOUBT THAT YOU CAN CHANGE HISTORY. YOU ALREADY HAVE. - MARGE PIERCY

480.

NOBODY REALLY CARES IF YOU'RE MISERABLE, SO YOU MIGHT AS WELL BE HAPPY. - CYNTHIA NELMS

481.

MONEY CAN'T BUY YOU HAPPINESS, BUT IT CAN BUY YOU A YACHT BIG ENOUGH TO PULL UP RIGHT ALONGSIDE IT. - DAVID LEE ROTH

482.

LET US REMEMBER - ONE BOOK, ONE PEN, ONE CHILD, AND ONE TEACHER CAN CHANGE THE WORLD. - MALALA YOUSAFZAI

483.

NEVER LOOK BACK UNLESS YOU ARE PLANNING TO GO THAT WAY. - HENRY DAVID THOREAU

484.

EVERY DAY IS A NEW DAY, AND YOU'LL NEVER BE ABLE TO FIND HAPPINESS IF YOU DON'T MOVE ON. - CARRIE UNDERWOOD

485.

I WANT TO TASTE AND GLORY IN EACH DAY, AND NEVER BE AFRAID TO EXPERIENCE PAIN. - SYLVIA PLATH

486.

THE INTELLIGENT USE OF SCIENCE AND TECHNOLOGY ARE THE TOOLS WITH WHICH TO ACHIEVE A NEW DIRECTION. - JACQUE FRESCO

487.

ONLY AN INVENTOR KNOWS HOW TO BORROW, AND EVERY MAN IS OR SHOULD BE AN INVENTOR. - RALPH WALDO EMERSON

488.

BLACK HISTORY IS PART OF AMERICAN HISTORY, AND IT SHOULD BE TREATED AS SUCH. - JANELLE MONAE

489.

PAINTING IS SELF DISCOVERY. EVERY GOOD ARTIST PAINTS WHAT HE IS.
- JACKSON POLLOCK

490.

ONE FRIEND IN A LIFETIME IS MUCH, TWO ARE MANY, THREE ARE HARDLY
POSSIBLE. - HENRY ADAMS

491.

THE ESSENCE OF TECHNOLOGY IS BY NO MEANS ANYTHING
TECHNOLOGICAL. - MARTIN HEIDEGGER

492.

WOMEN ARE THE REAL ARCHITECTS OF SOCIETY. - CHER

493.

MOST IMPORTANT THING IS TO TRY AND INSPIRE PEOPLE SO THAT THEY
CAN BE GREAT IN WHATEVER THEY WANT TO DO. - KOBE BRYANT

494.

THE DIGITAL REVOLUTION IS FAR MORE SIGNIFICANT THAN THE
INVENTION OF WRITING OR EVEN OF PRINTING. - DOUGLAS ENGELBART

495.

HAPPINESS DOES NOT CONSIST IN PASTIMES AND AMUSEMENTS BUT IN
VIRTUOUS ACTIVITIES. - ARISTOTLE

496.

IF YOU ARE AFRAID OF FAILURE YOU DON'T DESERVE TO BE
SUCCESSFUL. - CHARLES BARKLEY

497.

THE HAPPINESS OF YOUR LIFE DEPENDS UPON THE QUALITY OF YOUR THOUGHTS. THEREFORE,GUARD ACCORDINGLY. - MARCUS AURELIUS

498.

WE SHOULDN'T TEACH GREAT BOOKS. WE SHOULD TEACH A LOVE OF READING. - B. F. SKINNER

499.

DON'T WORRY ABOUT BEING A STAR, WORRY ABOUT DOING GOOD WORK, AND ALL THAT WILL COME TO YOU. - ICE CUBE

500.

WITHOUT PASSION YOU DON'T HAVE ENERGY, WITHOUT ENERGY YOU HAVE NOTHING. - DONALD TRUMP

NEXT BOOK

Cryptograms Puzzle Book for Adults

500+ Large Print Cryptogram Puzzles to Improve
Memory and Sharpen Brain

Go to the below URL:

www.bit.ly/stephenbooks

www.ingramcontent.com/pod-product-compliance
Lightning Source LLC
Chambersburg PA
CBHW081325120626
46546CB00011B/3221